MW01627619

TORAH
STUDIES

EDITOR
Rabbi Ahrele Loschak

CONTRIBUTING AUTHOR
Rabbi Eliezer Gurkow

ADMINISTRATOR
Rabbi Shlomie Tenenbaum

Printed in USA, 2023

THE ROHR JEWISH LEARNING INSTITUTE
832 Eastern Parkway, Brooklyn, NY 11213

(888) YOUR-JLI / (718) 221-6900
WWW.MYJLI.COM

ב"ה

SEASON THREE | YEAR 18 | BOOK 67

JLI

CELEBRATING 18 YEARS

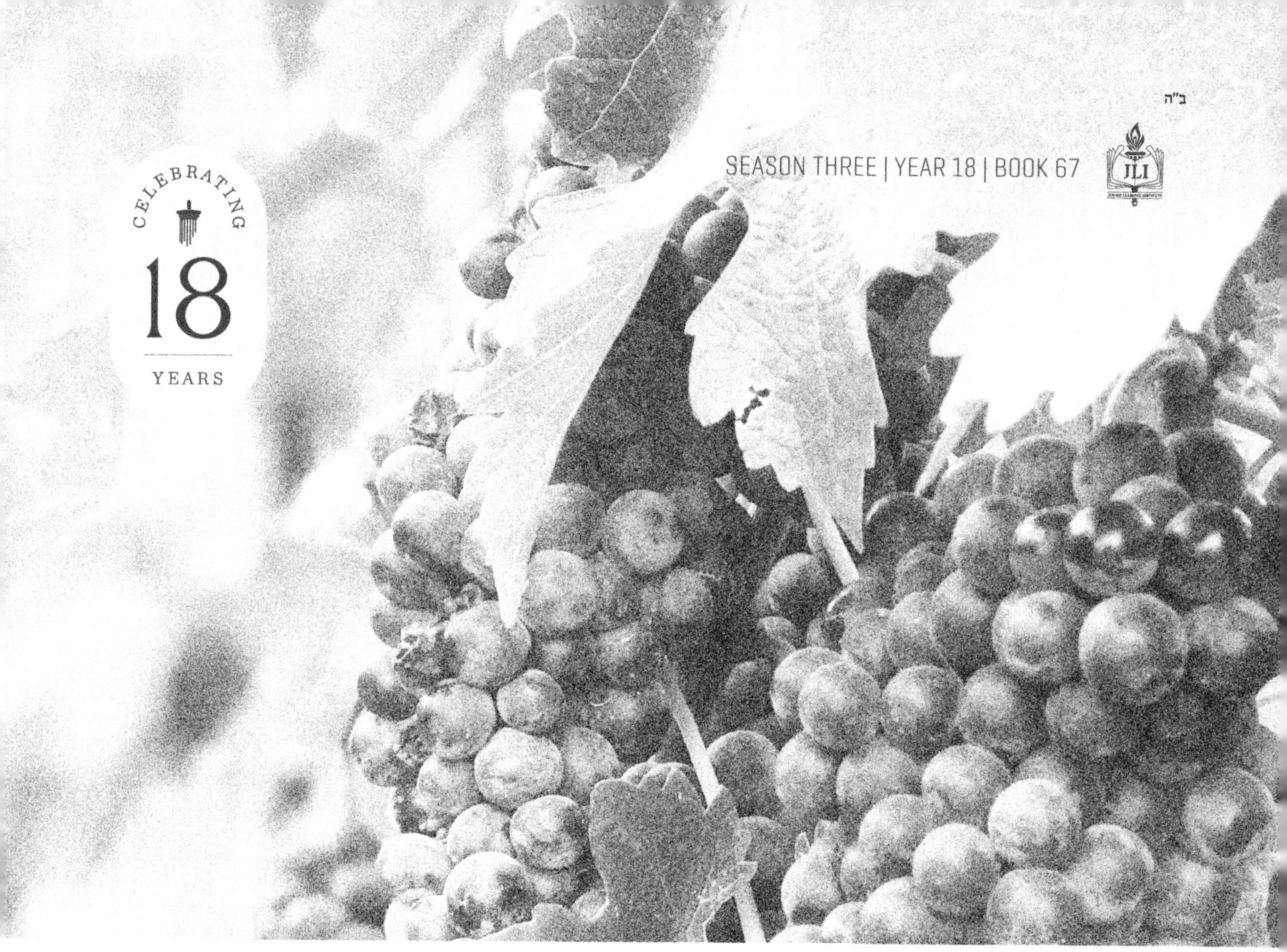

A WEEKLY JOURNEY INTO THE SOUL OF TORAH

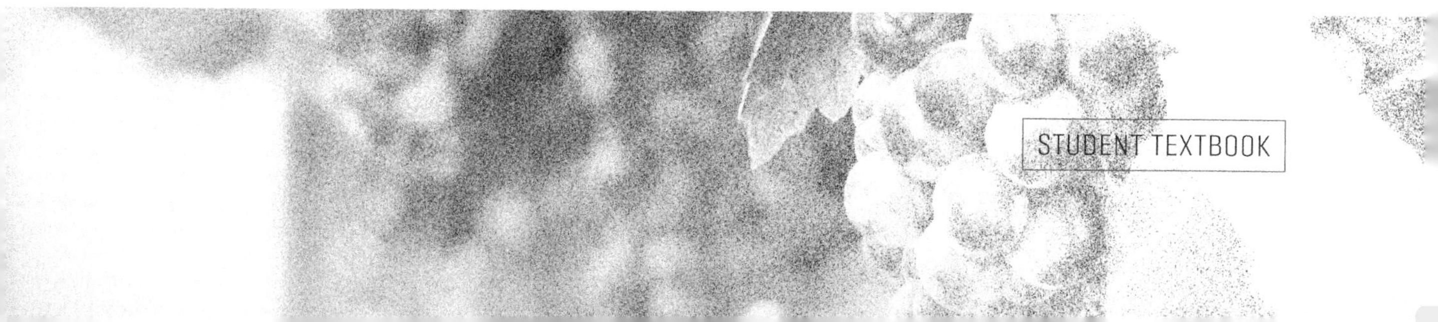

STUDENT TEXTBOOK

ADVISORY BOARD *of* GOVERNORS

Yaakov and Karen Cohen
Potomac, MD

Yitzchok and Julie Gniwisch
Montreal, QC

Barbara Hines
Aspen, CO

Ellen Marks
S. Diego, CA

David Mintz, OBM
Tenafly, NJ

George Rohr
New York, NY

Dr. Stephen F. Serbin
Columbia, SC

Leonard A. Wien, Jr.
Miami Beach, FL

PARTNERING FOUNDATIONS

Avi Chai Foundation

David Samuel Rock Foundation

Diamond Foundation

Estate of Elliot James Belkin

Francine Gani Charitable Fund

Goldstein Family Foundation

Harvey L. Miller Supporting Foundation

Kohelet Foundation

Kosins Family Foundation

Mayberg Foundation

Meromim Foundation

Myra Reinhard Family Foundation

Robbins Family Foundation

Ruderman Family Foundation

Schulich Foundation

William Davidson Foundation

World Zionist Organization

Yehuda and Anne Neuberger Philanthropic Fund

Zalik Foundation

PRINCIPAL BENEFACTOR

George Rohr
New York, NY

PILLARS *of* JEWISH LITERACY

Shaya and Sarah Boymelgreen
Miami Beach, FL

Pablo and Sara Briman
Mexico City, Mexico

Zalman and Mimi Fellig
Miami Beach, FL

Edwin and Arlene Goldstein
Cincinnati, OH

Yosef and Chana Malka Gorowitz
Redondo Beach, CA

Shloimy and Mirele Greenwald
Brooklyn, NY

Dr. Vera Koch Groszmann
S. Paulo, Brazil

Carolyn Hessel
New York, NY

Howard Jonas
Newark, NJ

David and Debra Magerman
Gladwyne, PA

Yitzchak Mirilashvili
Herzliya, Israel

David and Harriet Moldau
Longwood, FL

Ben Nash
New Jersey

Eyal and Aviva Postelnik
Marietta, GA

Clive and Zoe Rock
Irvine, CA

Michael and Fiona Scharf
Palm Beach, FL

Lee and Patti Schear
Dayton, OH

Isadore and Roberta Schoen
Fairfax, VA

Yair Shamir
Savyon, Israel

SPONSORS

Jake Aronov
Montgomery, AL

Moshe and Rebecca Bolinsky
Long Beach, NY

Daniel and Eta Cotlar
Houston, TX

Rabbi Meyer and Leah Eichler
Brooklyn, NY

Steve and Esther Feder
Los Angeles, CA

Yoel Gabay
Brooklyn, NY

Brian and Dana Gavin
Houston, TX

Shmuel and Sharone Goodman
Chicago, IL

Adam and Elisheva Hendry
Miami, FL

Michael and Andrea Leven
Atlanta, GA

Joe and Shira Lipsey
Aspen, CO

Josef Michelashvili
Glendale, NY

Harvey Miller
Chicago, IL

Rachelle Nedow
El Paso, TX

Peter and Hazel Pflaum
Newport Beach, CA

Abraham Podolak
Princeton Junction, NJ

Dr. Ze'ev and Varda Rav-Noy
Los Angeles, CA

Zvi Ryzman
Los Angeles, CA

Larry Sifen
Virginia Beach, VA

Myrna Zisman
Cedarhurst, NY

Janice and Ivan Zuckerman
Coral Gables, FL

THE ROHR JEWISH LEARNING INSTITUTE
gratefully acknowledges the pioneering support of

George and Pamela Rohr

Since its inception, the JLI has been a beneficiary of the vision, generosity, care, and concern of the Rohr family.

In the merit of the tens of thousands of hours of Torah study by JLI students worldwide, may they be blessed with health, *Yiddishe nachas* from all their loved ones, and extraordinary success in all their endeavors.

DEDICATED IN LOVING MEMORY OF AN EXTRAORDINARY WOMAN OF VALOR

Mrs. Golda Jacobs

חי׳ה גולדה בת ר׳ יעקב הכהן ז״ל

Her contagious positivity touched countless souls, and her light brightened and inspired. She was a graceful master of hospitality and a powerful force for promoting goodness.

May the merit of innumerable hours of Torah studied worldwide as a result of this course propel her soul ever higher through the brightest heavens and generate a fountain of blessings and solace to her family, in the form of abundant health, happiness, *nachas*, and success.

AND IN TRIBUTE
TO HER DEAR HUSBAND,

Martin Jacobs,

and their cherished children,

Zalmie, Yonina, Shoshana, and Dahlia

May her legacy of goodness forever continue to inspire them and their families to tread in her footsteps and carry further the spiritual torch that she held high.

Contents

1.

Tazria—Metzora

The Process of Redemption

News Flash: It's Already Underway

Dedicated in loving memory of Reb Mendel Drizin,
הרה"ח התמים ר' מנחם מענדל ע"ה בן הרב החסיד התמים מגדולי חסידי חב"ד ר' אברהם (מאיר) ז"ל,
marking his yahrzeit *on 19 Nisan,*
And in loving memory of his wife, Mrs. Channy Drizin,
חנה בילא גיצא ע"ה בת ר' ישראל משה ז"ל

May the merit of the Torah study worldwide accompany their souls in the world of everlasting life and be a source of blessings to their family, with much health, happiness, nachas, *and success.*

PARSHAH OVERVIEWS

Tazria-Metzora

The Torah portions of *Tazria* and *Metzora* continue the discussion of the laws of *tumah vetaharah*, ritual impurity and purity.

A woman who has given birth should undergo a process of purification, which includes immersing in a *mikveh* (a naturally gathered pool of water) and bringing offerings to the Holy Temple. All male infants are to be circumcised on the eighth day of life.

Tzaraat (often mistranslated as "leprosy") is a supranatural plague that can afflict people as well as garments or homes. If white or pink patches appear on a person's skin (dark pink or dark green in garments or homes), a *Kohen* is summoned. Judging by various signs, such as an increase in size of the afflicted area after a seven-day quarantine, the *Kohen* pronounces it *tamei* (impure) or *tahor* (pure).

A person afflicted with *tzaraat* must dwell alone outside of the camp (or city) until he or she is healed. The afflicted area in a garment or home must be removed; if the *tzaraat* recurs, the entire garment or home must be destroyed.

When the *metzora* (the person who has *tzaraat*) heals, he or she is purified by the *Kohen* with a special procedure involving two birds, spring water in an earthen vessel, a piece of cedar wood, a scarlet thread, and a bundle of hyssop.

Ritual impurity is also engendered through a seminal or other discharge in a man and menstruation or other discharge of blood in a woman, necessitating purification through immersion in a *mikveh*.

I. WHAT'S IN A NAME?

Two Portions, Two Odd Names

LEVITICUS 12:1–2

וַיְדַבֵּר ה' אֶל מֹשֶׁה וְאֶל אַהֲרֹן לֵאמֹר.

דַּבֵּר אֶל בְּנֵי יִשְׂרָאֵל לֵאמֹר, אִשָּׁה כִּי תַזְרִיעַ וְיָלְדָה.

G-d spoke to Moses and Aaron, saying:

Tell the Children of Israel, saying, 'If a woman conceives and gives birth . . .'"

Metzora—*The Second Portion*

TEXT 2

MIDRASH, *TANCHUMA*, *METZORA* 1

"זֹאת תִּהְיֶה תּוֹרַת הַמְּצֹרָע", אַל תִּקְרֵי הַמְּצֹרָע אֶלָּא הַמּוֹצִיא שֵׁם רָע.

אָמְרוּ רַבּוֹתֵינוּ זִכְרוֹנָם לִבְרָכָה: אֵין הַנְּגָעִים בָּאִים עַל הָאָדָם אֶלָּא עַל לָשׁוֹן הָרַע שֶׁמּוֹצִיא מִפִּיו. וְרוּחַ הַקֹּדֶשׁ צוֹוַחַת וְאוֹמֶרֶת לוֹ: "אַל תִּתֵּן אֶת פִּיךָ לַחֲטִיא אֶת בְּשָׂרְךָ" (קֹהֶלֶת ה, ה). אַל תִּתֵּן רְשׁוּת לְהוֹצִיא דָּבָר מִפִּיךָ לַחֲטִיא אֶת בְּשָׂרְךָ, לְהַלְקוֹת אֶת גּוּפְךָ.

This will be the law of the *metzora*. This word reads as an abbreviation for "*motzi shem ra*"—a slanderer.

Our sages of blessed memory said: These afflictions are brought upon us only because of the slander that issues from our mouths. The Sacred Spirit cries and proclaims, "Don't allow your mouth to bring sin to your flesh" (Ecclesiastes 5:5). Don't permit yourself to speak words that will stain your flesh [with *tzaraat* lesions] and harm your body.

Tanchuma

A Midrashic work bearing the name of Rabbi Tanchuma, a 4th-century Talmudic sage quoted often in this work. "Midrash" is the designation of a particular genre of rabbinic literature usually forming a running commentary on specific books of the Bible. *Tanchuma* provides textual exegeses, expounds upon the biblical narrative, and develops and illustrates moral principles. *Tanchuma* is unique in that many of its sections commence with a Halachic discussion, which subsequently leads into non-Halachic teachings.

TEXT 3

LEVITICUS 14:1–3

וַיְדַבֵּר ה' אֶל מֹשֶׁה וְאֶל אַהֲרֹן לֵאמֹר.

זֹאת תִּהְיֶה תּוֹרַת הַמְּצֹרָע בְּיוֹם טָהֳרָתוֹ, וְהוּבָא אֶל הַכֹּהֵן.

וְיָצָא הַכֹּהֵן אֶל מִחוּץ לַמַּחֲנֶה, וְרָאָה הַכֹּהֵן וְהִנֵּה נִרְפָּא נֶגַע הַצָּרַעַת מִן הַצָּרוּעַ.

And G-d spoke to Moses, saying:

"This should be the law of the *metzora* on the day of his cleansing: he should be brought to the priest (*Kohen*).

"The *Kohen* should leave the camp to see [the afflicted person] and, behold, the lesion of *tzaraat* has healed in the afflicted person."

II. ALTERNATIVE LOVE

What's in a Punishment?

TEXT 4

RABBI SHNEUR ZALMAN OF LIADI, *LIKUTEI TORAH*, PP. 53A; 86B

שהדין והמשפט הנמשך על החוטא מכורסייא דדינא זהו כמו רפואה לו, כמאמר: "מוטב דלידייניה וליתי לעלמא דאתי", שכדאי כל יסורי גיהנם כו'.

ולכן הדין . . . תכליתו חסד ולא נקמה חס ושלום . . .

ועל דרך זה גם כל עונשי התורה - עם היותן בחינת גבורות, מכל מקום הן כלולות בחסדים, שהעונש הוא שעל ידי זה נעשה תיקון לנפש החוטא.

Rabbi Shneur Zalman of Liadi (Alter Rebbe)
1745–1812

Chasidic rebbe, Halachic authority, and founder of the Chabad movement. The Alter Rebbe was born in Liozna, Belarus, and was among the principal students of the Magid of Mezeritch. His numerous works include the *Tanya*, an early classic containing the fundamentals of Chabad Chasidism; and *Shulchan Aruch HaRav,* an expanded and reworked code of Jewish law.

Punishment and judgment from the realm of justice are, in fact, a form of healing for the sinner. This is consistent with the rabbinic dictum, "It is better to be punished so that we can enter the World to Come [and receive our reward]" (Chagigah 15b). All our suffering is made worthwhile by this.

It follows that the ultimate purpose of punishment . . . is kindness, rather than revenge, G-d forbid. . . .

This is true of all the punishments in the Torah. Though they derive from a place of Divine discipline, they are, nevertheless, interlaced with kindness, for punishments cleanse the sinner's soul.

TEXT 5A

LEVITICUS 13:46

כָּל יְמֵי אֲשֶׁר הַנֶּגַע בּוֹ יִטְמָא, טָמֵא הוּא. בָּדָד יֵשֵׁב, מִחוּץ לַמַּחֲנֶה מוֹשָׁבוֹ.

So long as the lesions are upon him, the *metzora* is ritually impure. He is impure; he must remain isolated; his dwelling shall be outside of the camp.

TEXT 5B

RASHI, AD LOC.

"מִחוּץ לַמַּחֲנֶה". חוּץ לְשָׁלוֹשׁ מַחֲנוֹת.

"Outside of the camp." Outside of all three camps.

Rabbi Shlomo Yitzchaki (Rashi)
1040–1105

Most noted biblical and Talmudic commentator. Born in Troyes, France, Rashi studied in the famed *yeshivot* of Mainz and Worms. His commentaries on the Pentateuch and the Talmud, which focus on the straightforward meaning of the text, appear in virtually every edition of the Talmud and Bible.

TEXT 6

TALMUD, ARACHIN 16B

מה נשתנה מצורע שאמרה תורה: "בדד ישב, מחוץ למחנה מושבו" (ויקרא יג, מו)?

הוא הבדיל בין איש לאשתו בין איש לרעהו, לפיכך אמרה תורה: "בדד ישב".

Why is the *metzora* different in that he must "remain isolated; his dwelling shall be outside of the camp"?

His gossip created divisions between couples and friends. The Torah, therefore, decrees, "Remain isolated."

Babylonian Talmud

A literary work of monumental proportions that draws upon the legal, spiritual, intellectual, ethical, and historical traditions of Judaism. The 37 tractates of the Babylonian Talmud contain the teachings of the Jewish sages from the period after the destruction of the 2nd Temple through the 5th century CE. It has served as the primary vehicle for the transmission of the Oral Law and the education of Jews over the centuries; it is the entry point for all subsequent legal, ethical, and theological Jewish scholarship.

TEXT 7

MAIMONIDES, *MISHNEH TORAH,* LAWS OF *TZARAAT* IMPURITY 16:10

ויהיה מובדל ומפורסם לבדו, עד שלא יתעסק בשיחת הרשעים שהוא הליצנות ולשון הרע.

He is isolated, and it is made known that he must remain alone, so that he will not be involved in wicked talk—talk of mockery and of slander.

Rabbi Moshe ben Maimon (Maimonides, Rambam)
1135–1204

Halachist, philosopher, author, and physician. Maimonides was born in Córdoba, Spain. After the conquest of Córdoba by the Almohads, he fled Spain and eventually settled in Cairo, Egypt. There, he became the leader of the Jewish community and served as court physician to the vizier of Egypt. He is most noted for authoring the *Mishneh Torah*, an encyclopedic arrangement of Jewish law; and for his philosophical work, *Guide for the Perplexed*. His rulings on Jewish law are integral to the formation of Halachic consensus.

Explaining the Name Tazria

TEXT 8

THE REBBE, RABBI MENACHEM MENDEL SCHNEERSON, *LIKUTEI SICHOT* 22, P. 73

מהאי טעמא ווערט די פרשה אנגערופען "תזריע":

תזריע איז די התחלת הלידה פון חיים חדשים . . . (על דרך ווי זריעה בא תבואה ופירות - אז דערפון זאל נאכדעם קומען א נייע צמיחה).

אזוי איז דער תוכן ענין הנגעים פון פרשת תזריע: סיי דער נגע עצמו און סיי דער הסגר והחלט פון דעם מצורע וואס ער איז "מובדל ומפורסם לבדו" זיינען ניט . . . בתור עונש והעדר הטוב פאר דעם מצורע, כנזכר לעיל, נאר פרטים און מיטלען אין דעם תיקון (אין דער היילונג) פון דעם מצורע, אז ער זאל אריין אין א סדר פון חיים חדשים און ניט האבן קיין שייכות מיט "שיחת הרשעים שהוא הליצנות ולשון הרע".

This is why the Torah portion is named "*Tazria*—conception."

Conception is the beginning of birth and new life (similar to planting a seed to initiate new growth).

This captures the intent of the lesions in this Torah portion. The lesions, and the isolation that follows, in which the *metzora* is alone and it is made known that he is alone, are not meant to punish and deprive. Rather, they are steps and methods to rectify (and thus heal) the *metzora*. They help him enter a new life with no inappropriate or evil speech.

Rabbi Menachem Mendel Schneerson 1902–1994

The towering Jewish leader of the 20th century, known as "the Lubavitcher Rebbe," or simply as "the Rebbe." Born in southern Ukraine, the Rebbe escaped Nazi-occupied Europe, arriving in the U.S. in June 1941. The Rebbe inspired and guided the revival of traditional Judaism after the European devastation, impacting virtually every Jewish community the world over. The Rebbe often emphasized that the performance of just one additional good deed could usher in the era of Mashiach. The Rebbe's scholarly talks and writings have been printed in more than 200 volumes.

Explaining the Name Metzora

TEXT 9

THE REBBE, RABBI MENACHEM MENDEL SCHNEERSON, IBID., P. 75

על פי זה איז אויך מבואר דער שם פון דער צווייטער סדרה, "מצורע", כאטש דארט רעדט זיך ניט ווי דער מצורע איז במצב של טומאה, נאר ווי ער איז "ביום טהרתו":

דערמיט ווערט ארויסגעבראכט, אז טהרת (ורפואת) המצורע (המבוארת בפרשת מצורע) איז ניט קיין באזונדער אויפטו, וואס ווערט נתחדש (בלויז) מצד די פעולות וקרבנות וועלכע זיינען מבואר אין דער פרשה, נאר דאס אלץ קומט בהמשך און אלס מסובב פון די ענינים המבוארים בפרשת תזריע.

בסגנון אחר: די פעולות שבפרשת מצורע וואס טוען אויף די טהרה (בפועל), זיינען (בלויז) ממשיך ומגלה דאס וואס האט זיך שוין אויפגעטאן אין דעם אדם דורך דער צרעת גופא . . . די רפואת האדם ברוחניות (וואס דאס איז די סיבת הצרעת) איז דורך דער צרעת והסגר ("בדד ישב גו'").

און דעריבער ווערט די פרשה ניט אנגערופן "ביום טהרתו" (וכיוצא בזה) וואס וואלט אנגעדייטעט אז דוקא דא טוט זיך אויף טהרתו, נאר דוקא "מצורע" וואס ברענגט ארויס אז דאס איז די תוצאה פון דעם ענין ה"מצורע" גופא.

This also explains why our second Torah portion is called *Metzora* despire the fact that it discusses the *metzora*'s state of purification rather than his previous impure state.

This underscores the fact that the *metzora*'s (healing) and purification (delineated in this Torah portion) are not a new development achieved by the methods and offerings described in this portion. Rather, they are all linked to, and caused by, the subjects discussed in the previous portion.

Another way of putting it: The steps outlined in this Torah portion that render the *metzora* (factually) pure (merely) draw out and reveal what the ailment accomplished. . . . The spiritual healing (which was the purpose of the ailment) was already accomplished by the lesions and the quarantine.

Therefore, the name of this Torah portion is not "on the day of his purification" because this would have implied that his purification was first achieved at this point. Rather it is called *Metzora* to underscore that the purification [begins with and] emerges from the ailment.

III. MASHIACH IN THE MAKING

In the Oven

TEXT 10A

GENESIS 1:2

וְהָאָרֶץ הָיְתָה תֹהוּ וָבֹהוּ וְחֹשֶׁךְ עַל פְּנֵי תְהוֹם, וְרוּחַ אֱלֹקִים מְרַחֶפֶת עַל פְּנֵי הַמָּיִם.

The earth was astonishingly empty, and darkness was on the face of the deep, and the spirit of G-d was hovering over the face of the water.

TEXT 10B

MIDRASH, *BERESHIT RABAH*, AD LOC.

"וְרוּחַ אֱלֹקִים מְרַחֶפֶת", זֶה רוּחוֹ שֶׁל מֶלֶךְ הַמָּשִׁיחַ.

"The spirit of G-d was hovering"—this is the spirit of Mashiach.

Bereshit Rabah

An early rabbinic commentary on the Book of Genesis. This Midrash bears the name of Rabbi Oshiya Rabah (Rabbi Oshiya "the Great"), whose teaching opens this work. This Midrash provides textual exegeses and stories, expounds upon the biblical narrative, and develops and illustrates moral principles. Produced by the sages of the Talmud in the Land of Israel, its use of Aramaic closely resembles that of the Jerusalem Talmud. It was first printed in Constantinople in 1512 together with 4 other Midrashic works on the other 4 books of the Pentateuch.

An Analogy

TEXT 11

RABBI SHNEUR ZALMAN OF LIADI, *TORAH OR*, P. 55A

הנה הגלות נמשל לעבור, וגאולת ימי המשיח שיהיה במהרה בימינו נמשל ללידה, כמו שכתוב: "כי חלה גם ילדה ציון את בניה" (ישעיהו סו, ח). וכשישראל נתונים בצרה, חס ושלום, כתיב: "כי באו בנים עד משבר וכח אין ללידה" (שם לז, ג). וכן חבלי ימות המשיח נקראים בשם חבלי לידה, כמו שכתוב: "כי חבלי לידה יבאו לך" (הושע יג, יג) . . .

דהיינו שיש להעובר כל חיתוך האיברים, ראש, ועינים, ואזנים כו'. אלא שראשו מקופל ומונח בין ברכיו, שאינו משמש כלום, שאינו מחשב ומהרהר. וכן עיניים לו ולא יראה, ואזניים ולא ישמע. וגם המאכל שלו, אף שאוכל ממה שאמו אוכלת, אינו הולך לו דרך הפה, רק דרך הטבור לבני מעיים בלבד להגדיל הגוף. כמו שנראה בחוש שבתשעה ירחי לידה נגדל גופו . . . ויש בו אברי הנשימה גם כן, מכל מקום, הרי אין לו נשמת רוח חיים עד שיצא לאויר העולם . . .

והנה ככל הדברים האלה וככל המשל הזה, כך נמשלו בני ישראל בעת הגלות . . . דסליק קודשא בריך הוא לעילא . . . פירוש שסילק שכינתו וגילוי אלקותו מהתחתונים, ודומה לעיני בשר כאלו העולם דבר בפני עצמו . . .

והנה תכלית השלימות של ימות המשיח, שהוא בחינת לידה והתגלות אור ה' בקרב איש ולב עמוק.

The Exile may be compared to a fetus. The Redemption that we will soon experience may be compared to birth, as the passage states, "Zion prevailed and gave birth to her sons" (Isaiah 66:8). When Jews are in trouble, G-d forfend, it is like "the children have reached the birth stage, but lack the strength to give birth" (Isaiah 37:3). Similarly, the sufferings we experience just prior to the Redemption can be compared to birth pangs, as the passage states, "Pangs of childbirth assail you" (Hosea 13:13). . . .

A fetus has all its limbs, head, eyes, ears, etc. However, they don't function. The brain can't think, the eyes can't see, the ears can't hear. Although it eats from its mother's food, the food doesn't enter through the mouth, but rather directly into the stomach through the umbilical cord. The body is completely developed, as is readily visible during the final month of pregnancy. . . . It even has lungs; however, it doesn't breathe until it enters the world. . . .

This is a perfect analogy for the Jewish people before the messianic era—a time when G-d withdraws to the celestial realm. . . . This means that G-d withdraws His revealed presence from the lower realm to the extent that it appears as if the world exists without G-d. . . .

The absolute perfection that we will achieve in the messianic era is the birth and revelation of G-d's light in the hidden depths of our hearts.

TEXT 12

THE REBBE, RABBI MENACHEM MENDEL SCHNEERSON,
TORAT MENACHEM 5713:2 (7), P. 132

מבלי הבט על גודל החושך מצד הקליפות . . . צריך לידע שישנו כבר "רוחו של מלך המשיח". על דרך שמצינו במדרשי חכמינו זכרונם לברכה בנוגע לחורבן בית המקדש, שתיכף ומיד נולד מושיען של ישראל.

אלא שצריכים רק לגלות זאת.

Notwithstanding the great spiritual darkness of our times, . . . we must know that the spirit of Mashiach is already present. As our sages of blessed memory taught, Mashiach was born the moment the Temple was destroyed.

However, it is up to us to reveal this.

TEXT 13A

THE REBBE, RABBI MENACHEM MENDEL SCHNEERSON, *LIKUTEI SICHOT* 22, PP. 75–76

די עבודה פון אידן בזמן הגלות איז אן ענין פון "תזריע" – א זריעה והכרח לצמיחה והתחלת הצמיחה בזמן פון דער גאולה . . .

דאס הייסט, אז דאס וואס עס טוט זיך אויף לימות המשיח ותחיית המתים איז ניט קיין באזונדער זאך פון ענין הגלות, נאר דאס איז די "צמיחה", וואס "וואקסט אויס" פון עבודת ה"זריעה" בזמן הגלות.

Our work during the Exile is akin to planting—a necessary step that initiates a sprouting and growth at the time of our Redemption. . . .

This means that what will occur in the messianic era is not separate from what occurs today. Rather, it is an outgrowth from the planting that we do today in Exile.

TEXT 13B

THE REBBE, RABBI MENACHEM MENDEL SCHNEERSON, IBID.

איז אויך דעם די הוראה, אז . . . אין "מעשינו ועבודתינו" פון זמן הגלות דארף דערהערט ווערן אז דאס איז אן ענין פון "תזריע" וואס ברענגט די "צמיחה", דעם גילוי פון משיח צדקנו.

ובמילא, אז די גילויים דלעתיד זיינען ניט קיין באזונדער ענין, נאר א המשך ותוצאה פון דער עבודה פון גלות . . . די צמיחה וואס קומט פון דער עבודה אין גלות.

The lesson is that we must view our efforts and devotions during the period of Exile as planting seeds that will trigger the sprouting of the messianic era and the Divine revelations we will enjoy then.

This means that the messianic era of the future is not separate from today's devotions. Rather, it is a continuation and outcome from our devotion to G-d today. It is the growth that results from our current efforts.

A Blend, Not Cause and Effect

TEXT 14

THE REBBE, RABBI MENACHEM MENDEL SCHNEERSON, IBID., P. 77

דאס גופא קען זיין אויף צוויי אופנים:

א) ער דערהערט ווי זיין עבודה, "תזריע", איז א זריעה וואס וועט ברענגען די צמיחה, די גאולה, אבער דאס איז . . . אלס נאך א זאך, וואס וועט זיין בנפרד. ער האלט טאקע בא "אחכה לו בכל יום שיבוא", און די עבודה איז צוליב דעם "שיבוא" – בא אים הערט זיך דאס אבער ווי נאך אן ענין, אז דורך מעשינו ועבודתינו ברענגט מען אראפ און מ'איז ממהר (א באזונדער ענין) ביאת משיח צדקנו . . .

ב) א העכערער אופן איז, אז בא אים איז "תזריע ומצורע" מחוברות – דער אחכה און קווינו כל היום . . . אין זיין עבודת "תזריע", איז ניט נאר אז יעדע זיין עבודה וועט גלייך גורם זיין "שיבוא", נאר אז די גאולה העתידה איז איין זאך מיט תוכן עבודתו ("תזריע מצורע" ווערן איין פרשה) – ווייל ביאת המשיח איז די צמיחה ובמילא די שלימות פון זיין זריעה.

This can occur in two ways:

A. We realize that our efforts plant seeds that will result in the Redemption, but the result seems separate from our efforts. We await Mashiach imminently and work to hasten his revelation; however, our efforts and his revelation feel like two separate stages. (1) Our efforts (2) hasten his revelation. . . .

B. A better approach is to combine the two, as in when the Torah portions *Tazria* and *Metzora* are combined. This means that we don't just plant seeds by awaiting, ancitipating, and working to hasten the revelation of Mashiach. Rather, his coming becomes part of our effort—*Tazria* and *Metzora*, a single continuum. Mashiach's arrival is the result, and therefore the culimation, of our efforts.

Living with Mashiach

TEXT 15

THE REBBE, RABBI MENACHEM MENDEL SCHNEERSON,
TORAT MENACHEM 5719:2 (25), P. 208

> שמעתי מאבי אדוני ומורי, זכרונו לברכה, ביאור דיוק הלשון "להביא לימות המשיח", . . . שצריכים "להביא" (אריינברייינגען) את הגילוי דימות המשיח גם עכשיו בעולם הזה.

I heard from my father and mentor of blessed memory that our sages' statement—"To bring the messianic era"—. . . tells us to bring (introduce) Mashiach into our present.

KEY POINTS

» The *metzora*'s quarantine and impure lesions are not separate from their eventual purification. They are part of the same process. The process of purification begins with being declared impure.

» The same is true of every trouble in life. The solution begins the moment we become aware of the problem. They are not two stages. The problem and solution are a single process.

» This applies to Exile and Redemption. Our *mitzvot* during the Exile bring about our Redemption. But they are not two stages, one triggered by the other. They are a single continuum. Mashiach is already here. Like a fetus in the womb, we need time to be ready.

» When we realize this, Mashiach becomes an imminent part of our daily reality. We think about him, learn about him, and are excited about his arrival. We act as if he is already here.

» This mindset ensures that when someone talks about Mashiach, we don't view it as a pipe dream. We see it as a reality that has already begun and will soon announce itself.

2.

Acharei Mot—Kedoshim

Children Are Small Adults

It's Never Too Early to Start a Jewish Education

Dedicated to Ellen Marks as she marks her birthday on 30 Nissan, and with deep appreciation for her ongoing friendship and partnership with JLI.

May she go from strength to strength and enjoy good health, happiness, nachas *from her loved ones, and success in all her endeavors.*

PARSHAH OVERVIEWS

Acharei Mot

Following the deaths of Nadab and Abihu, G-d warns against unauthorized entry "into the Holy." Only one person, the *Kohen Gadol* (High Priest), once a year on Yom Kippur, may enter the innermost chamber in the Sanctuary to offer the sacred *ketoret* to G-d.

Another feature of the Day of Atonement service is the casting of lots over two goats, to determine which should be offered to G-d and which should be dispatched to carry off the sins of Israel to the wilderness.

The *parshah* of *Acharei Mot* also warns against bringing *korbanot* (animal or meal offerings) anywhere but in the Holy Temple, forbids the consumption of blood, and details the laws prohibiting incest and other forbidden sexual relations.

Kedoshim

The *parshah* of *Kedoshim* begins with the statement: "You shall be holy, for I, the L-rd your G-d, am holy." This is followed by dozens of *mitzvot* (Divine commandments) through which the Jew sanctifies him- or herself and relates to the holiness of G-d.

These include: the prohibition against idolatry; the mitzvah of charity; the principle of equality before the law; and the laws regarding Shabbat, sexual morality, honesty in business, honor and awe of one's parents, and the sacredness of life.

Also in *Kedoshim* is the dictum, "Love your fellow as yourself," which the great sage Rabbi Akiva called "a central principle of Torah," and about which Hillel said, "This is the entire Torah; the rest is commentary."

INTRODUCTION

Exercise

Take a look at this meme.

Why is it absurd? What's wrong about the parent's approach here?

____

____

____

I. CELEBRATING THE PREP

Sefirah: *Countdown to the Torah*

TEXT 1

LEVITICUS 23:15–16

טו. וּסְפַרְתֶּם לָכֶם מִמָּחֳרַת הַשַּׁבָּת, מִיּוֹם הֲבִיאֲכֶם אֶת עֹמֶר הַתְּנוּפָה, שֶׁבַע שַׁבָּתוֹת תְּמִימֹת תִּהְיֶינָה:

טז. עַד מִמָּחֳרַת הַשַּׁבָּת הַשְּׁבִיעִת תִּסְפְּרוּ חֲמִשִּׁים יוֹם, וְהִקְרַבְתֶּם מִנְחָה חֲדָשָׁה לַה':

15. And you shall count for yourselves, from the morrow of the rest day, from the day you bring the *Omer* as a wave offering, seven weeks; they shall be complete.

16. You shall count until the day after the seventh week, [namely] the fiftieth day, [on which] you shall bring a new meal offering to G-d.

TEXT 2

RABBI SHNEUR ZALMAN OF LIADI, *SHULCHAN ARUCH HARAV, ORACH CHAYIM* 489:1

מצות עשה מן התורה שיספור כל אחד מישראל שבעה שבועות ימים מיום הבאת קרבן העומר . . . ודרשו חכמים: "תספר לך", יכול בבית דין כמו ביובל - שסופרין בבית דין שבע שבתות שנים ומקדשין שנת החמשים ליובל? תלמוד לומר: "וספרתם לכם", כדי לספורה לכל אחד ואחד. ואין הציבור או שליח צבור יכולים לספור בעד כולם.

It is a biblical mitzvah for every Jew to count on a daily basis for seven weeks, starting from when the *Omer* sacrifice is offered. The sages interpreted the words, "Count for yourselves": It might be thought that it is the Jewish court who conducts this count, in the same way that the Jewish court counts the seven-year cycles and then sanctifies the fiftieth year as the jubilee year. But "count for yourself" teaches us that every person must do the count. The congregation and the leaders are unable to count on behalf of the public.

Rabbi Shneur Zalman of Liadi (Alter Rebbe)
1745–1812

Chasidic rebbe, Halachic authority, and founder of the Chabad movement. The Alter Rebbe was born in Liozna, Belarus, and was among the principal students of the Magid of Mezeritch. His numerous works include the *Tanya*, an early classic containing the fundamentals of Chabad Chasidism; and *Shulchan Aruch HaRav*, an expanded and reworked code of Jewish law.

TEXT 3

MIDRASH, CITED BY RABBI YITZCHAK TYRNAU, *SEFER HAMINHAGIM*

ולמה מונים ספירה מפסח ועד עצרת יותר מבשאר מועדים?

משל למה הדבר דומה? לשר אחד שרכב בדרך ומצא אדם אחד מושלך בבור שהיה אסור שם. אמר לו השר: אני אעלה אותך ואוציא אותך מהבור הזה, ולזמן פלוני אתן לך את ביתי. שמח אותו אדם שמחה גדולה ואמר: לא די שמוציאני מהבור הזה, אלא עדיין רוצה לתת לי את בתו. וכך עשה השר: הוציאו מהבור והלבישו בגדים נאים כסף וזהב נתן לו.

וכשראה אותו האיש כך שהשר קיים מקצת דבריו, התחיל למנות מיד כמה זמן יש למה שקבע לו השר לתת לו בתו . . .

כך היו ישראל במצרים כמו בבור וכו'.

Why do we count the days between Pesach and Shavuos, more so than any other festival?

This can be compared to a prince who was out riding and found a man who had been cast into a pit. The prince told him, "I will pull you out of this pit, and then after some time, I will give you my daughter as a wife." The man grew tremendously happy and said to himself, "Not only will he take me out of this pit but he also wants to give me his daughter!" And the prince did just that. He took the fellow out of the pit, dressed him in fine clothes, and gave him gold and silver.

When the man saw that the prince was true to his word, he began to count how long it would be until the prince would fulfill his pledge to give him his daughter. . . .

The Jews in Egypt were as if in a pit.

Question: Why Mark the In-Between?

TEXT 4

RABBI MORDECHAI YOFFE, *LEVUSH HACHUR, ORACH CHAYIM* 489:1

ואין מברכין זמן על הספירה . . . משום שטעם הספירה הוא שציוונו ה׳ יתברך לספור שבועות וימים עד יום חמישים יום שיצאו ממצרים, שבו יהיה מתן תורה, כאדם המצפה וממתין על יום המוגבל לו לתת מתנה מרובה או דבר אחר שישמח בו, ומקווה ומייחל מתי יהיה אותו היום שיקבל אותה הטובה המיועדת לו, ובכל יום שישקע השמש הוא סופר ומברך לאלקיו שעבר זה היום ומתקרב אותו היום אשר חפץ בו.

וכן ציווה ה׳ יתברך לספור כל הימים והשבועות עד היום שקיוינוהו, הוא יום מתן תורתנו, לחבב עלינו את התורה ולהראות שהיא חביבה עלינו יותר מיום הגאולה של מצרים והוא עיקר היום שקיוינוהו.

ואם כן הספירה הוא בעבור תוחלת הממושכה שאנו מראים שיאריך לנו הזמן עד יום מתן תורה, ובכל יום אנו מברכין ומשבחין שהגיע אותו היום ונתקרב יום מתן תורה.

ואם כן, איך נברך זמן על הספירה, ועדיין לא הגיע היום שקיוינוהו שהוא עיקר השמחה, שהוא מתן תורה? שהרי אין מברכין זמן אלא על דבר ששמחין בו, ובספירה אין בה שמחה, לכך אין מברכין זמן.

We do not recite the Shehecheyanu blessing when counting *sefirah*: . . . The reason for counting fifty days is because G-d commanded us to count the fifty days from the Exodus from Egypt to the day we would receive the Torah as one who's waiting for a designated day when they're scheduled to receive a great gift or some other joyful thing. This person would hope and be anxious for that day to finally arrive. Every day when the sun sets, they count the days gone and bless G-d that [this day] has passed and they're one day closer to the anticipated day.

Rabbi Mordechai Yoffe
1530–1612

Student of Rabbi Moshe Isserlis; served as rabbi in Prague, Lublin, Hurdna, and Posen. He was one of the leaders of the Council of Four Lands, a central body of Jewish authority in Poland. He authored the *Levush*, a code of law that is more comprehensive than the concise style of the Shulchan Aruch.

So, too, G-d commanded us to count all the days and weeks leading up to the anticipated day—the day when the Torah would be given. The purpose of this is to increase our love for the Torah and to show how it is dearer to us even than the day we left Egypt. It is the primary day we anticipated.

Accordingly, *sefirah* is about the upcoming goal, demonstrating how time is passing until we reach the day the Torah will be given. Each day, we bless and praise G-d that another day has passed and brought us closer to receiving the Torah.

Accordingly, how can we make the Shehecheyanu blessing when counting *sefirah*, when the desired day and primary cause of joy, *Matan Torah*, hasn't yet arrived? After all, we only recite Shehecheyanu for a joyous occasion, whereas with *sefirah*, there is no joy. Thus, we don't recite the Shehecheyanu blessing.

II. THE MITZVAH OF *CHINUCH*

A Minor Role

TEXT 5

TALMUD, SUKKAH 42A

תנו רבנן: קטן היודע לנענע, חייב בלולב. להתעטף, חייב בציצית. לשמור תפילין, אביו לוקח לו תפילין. יודע לדבר, אביו לומדו תורה וקריאת שמע.

תורה מאי היא? אמר רב המנונא: "תורה צוה לנו משה מורשה קהלת יעקב". קריאת שמע מאי היא? פסוק ראשון.

The sages taught: a minor who knows how to wave the *lulav* is obligated in the mitzvah of *lulav*; one who knows how to wrap himself in a garment is obligated in the mitzvah of *tzitzit*; if he knows to preserve the sanctity of *tefilin* in a state of cleanliness, his father buys him *tefilin*; if he knows how to speak, his father immediately teaches him Torah and Shema.

What [part of the] Torah is taught to such a child? Rav Hamnuna said, "The verse, 'Moses commanded us Torah, an inheritance of the congregation of Jacob'" (Deuteronomy 33:4). And what [part of the] Shema is taught to such a child? The first verse of Shema.

Babylonian Talmud

A literary work of monumental proportions that draws upon the legal, spiritual, intellectual, ethical, and historical traditions of Judaism. The 37 tractates of the Babylonian Talmud contain the teachings of the Jewish sages from the period after the destruction of the 2nd Temple through the 5th century CE. It has served as the primary vehicle for the transmission of the Oral Law and the education of Jews over the centuries; it is the entry point for all subsequent legal, ethical, and theological Jewish scholarship.

TEXT 6

RABBI SHLOMO BEN ADERET, MEGLLAH 19B

דכולי עלמא אין הקטן מוציא אף על גב שהגיע לחינוך. והנכון דקטן שהגיע לחינוך אינו מחוייב במצות כלל ואפילו מדרבנן, אלא שאנו מצווין עליו לחנכו במצות . . . ולפיכך אינו ראוי להוציא אחרים אפילו במצות דרבנן, שכל שאינו מחויב בדבר אינו מוציא אחרים ידי חובתן.

It is unanimous that a minor cannot discharge another person's obligation, even if they have reached a mature age. This is a correct ruling, for a mature minor is not obligated to fulfill any *mitzvot*, even by rabbinic standards. It is *we* who are obligated to educate the minor in mitzvah performance. . . . Therefore, it doesn't make sense for a minor to discharge anyone else's obligation, even for a rabbinic mitzvah, for anyone who isn't obligated themselves cannot discharge someone else's obligation.

Rabbi Shlomo ben Aderet (Rashba)
1235–1310

Medieval Halachist, Talmudist, and philosopher. Rashba was born in Barcelona, Spain, and was a student of Nachmanides and Rabbi Yonah of Gerona. He was known as El Rab d'España ("the rav of Spain") because of his fame as a rabbinical authority. More than 3,000 of his responsa are extant, dealing with varied questions on Halachah and religious philosophy, addressed to him from Spain, Portugal, Italy, France, Germany, and Asia Minor. Among his numerous students were the Ritva, Rabbeinu Bechaye, and the Re'ah.

A Major Role?

TEXT 7A

MAIMONIDES, *MISHNEH TORAH*, LAWS OF TORAH STUDY 1:2-3

> וְחַיָּב לִשְׂכֹּר מְלַמֵּד לִבְנוֹ לְלַמְּדוֹ, וְאֵינוֹ חַיָּב לְלַמֵּד בֶּן חֲבֵרוֹ אֶלָּא בְּחִנָּם.
> מִי שֶׁלֹּא לִמְּדוֹ אָבִיו - חַיָּב לְלַמֵּד אֶת עַצְמוֹ כְּשֶׁיַּכִּיר, שֶׁנֶּאֱמַר: "וּלְמַדְתֶּם אֹתָם וּשְׁמַרְתֶּם לַעֲשֹׂתָם".

One is obligated to hire a teacher for one's son, while one is not required to undertake any expense to teach a colleague's son.

A person who was not instructed by his father is obligated to arrange for his own instruction when he can understand, as the verse states, "And you shall study them and take heed to perform them" (Deuteronomy 5:1).

Rabbi Moshe ben Maimon (Maimonides, Rambam)
1135–1204

Halachist, philosopher, author, and physician. Maimonides was born in Córdoba, Spain. After the conquest of Córdoba by the Almohads, he fled Spain and eventually settled in Cairo, Egypt. There, he became the leader of the Jewish community and served as court physician to the vizier of Egypt. He is most noted for authoring the *Mishneh Torah*, an encyclopedic arrangement of Jewish law; and for his philosophical work, *Guide for the Perplexed*. His rulings on Jewish law are integral to the formation of Halachic consensus.

TEXT 7B

RABBI MENACHEM MENDEL OF LUBAVITCH, *CHIDUSHEI TZEMACH TZEDEK, PISKEI DINIM, CHIDUSHIM AL HARAMBAM*, P. 1

> יש לומר כיון דתלמוד תורה . . . מחויב האב מדאורייתא ללמוד את בנו . . . אם כן שמא גם על הקטן יש חיוב מדאורייתא.

Inasmuch as the father is Scripturally obligated to teach his son Torah, . . . it may be suggested that . . . a Scriptural obligation lies on the minor as well.

Rabbi Menachem Mendel of Lubavitch (*Tzemach Tzedek*)
1789–1866

Chasidic rebbe and noted author. The *Tzemach Tzedek* was the third leader of the Chabad Chasidic movement and a noted authority on Jewish law. His numerous works include Halachic responsa, Chasidic discourses, and kabbalistic writings. Active in the communal affairs of Russian Jewry, he worked to alleviate the plight of the cantonists, Jewish children kidnapped to serve in the czar's army. He passed away in Lubavitch, leaving seven sons and two daughters.

TEXT 8

MAIMONIDES, *MISHNEH TORAH*, LAWS OF BLESSINGS 5:15

> שְׁנַיִם שֶׁאָכְלוּ כְּאֶחָד, כָּל אֶחָד וְאֶחָד מְבָרֵךְ לְעַצְמוֹ. וְאִם הָיָה אֶחָד מֵהֶן יוֹדֵעַ וְאֶחָד אֵינוֹ יוֹדֵעַ - זֶה שֶׁיּוֹדֵעַ מְבָרֵךְ בְּקוֹל רָם, וְהַשֵּׁנִי עוֹנֶה אָמֵן אַחַר כָּל בְּרָכָה וּבְרָכָה וְיוֹצֵא יְדֵי חוֹבָתוֹ. וּבֵן מְבָרֵךְ לְאָבִיו.

When two people eat together, each person should recite Grace after Meals by himself. If one knows how to recite Grace and the other does not, the one who knows should recite the Grace out loud, and the other person should recite *amen* after each blessing. In this manner, the one who doesn't know the prayer fulfills his obligation. A son may recite Grace for his father.

TEXT 9A

THE REBBE, RABBI MENACHEM MENDEL SCHNEERSON, *LIKUTEI SICHOT* 17, P. 235

> איז ניט מובן: ווי קען מען זאגן א חיוב אויף א קטן אפילו מדרבנן, וויבאלד ער איז ניט קיין בר דיעה, ובלשון הגמרא "חיובא לדרדקי (בתמיה)"?

It's puzzling: How can we suggest that an obligation rests on a minor, even by rabbinic standards, if the minor lacks maturity? As the Talmud (Pesachim 116a) phrases it, "An obligation for a minor?!"

Rabbi Menachem Mendel Schneerson 1902–1994

The towering Jewish leader of the 20th century, known as "the Lubavitcher Rebbe," or simply as "the Rebbe." Born in southern Ukraine, the Rebbe escaped Nazi-occupied Europe, arriving in the U.S. in June 1941. The Rebbe inspired and guided the revival of traditional Judaism after the European devastation, impacting virtually every Jewish community the world over. The Rebbe often emphasized that the performance of just one additional good deed could usher in the era of Mashiach. The Rebbe's scholarly talks and writings have been printed in more than 200 volumes.

Yes, a Major Role

TEXT 9B

THE REBBE, RABBI MENACHEM MENDEL SCHNEERSON, IBID., PP. 236–237

די שייכות והשתתפות פון קטן אין דער מצות חינוך באשטייט ניט (בלויז) אין דעם וואס אן דעם קטן – קען דער אב ניט מקיים זיין מצות החינוך, נאר (אויך וואס) דאס איז די מצוה – (דער אב זאל מחנך זיין אז דער בן זאל טאן די *מצוה*; און דעריבער . . . וויבאלד אבער אז די מצות האב איז לחנך אז דער בן זאל מקיים זיין די מצוה, ווערט בדרך ממילא אויפן בן א התחייבות אינעם קיום פון די מצוות, הייסט אויך דער בן א *מחויב* בדבר.

בסגנון אחר: וויבאלד אז דער אב איז מחויב צו מחנך זיין את בנו לעשות המצוה, איז כאטש אז עשיית הבן את המצוה איז מצד דעם (חיוב וואס איז *מוטל על ה*)אב – איז דאס אבער דאך פעולת המצוה (בשלימות) על ידי *הקטן* מצד ציווי (שעל האב), און דעריבער הייסט דער קטן א מחויב בדבר, ביז אז ער איז מוציא א גדול.

Let's understand the role and part the minor plays in the mitzvah of education. He is not just an actor without whom the father wouldn't be able to fulfill *his* (the father's) mitzvah of education. Rather, the minor is the subject of the mitzvah of education, as the mitzvah is for the minor to gain practice. . . . So, inasmuch as the father's mitzvah is to educate the child to perform all *mitzvot*, a sense of responsibility automatically lands on the minor, and that renders the minor a "responsible party."

In other words: The father is obligated to educate his child to perform *mitzvot*. Though the minor's mitzvah performance is an outgrowth of the *father's* obligation, it is the act of the mitzvah performed *by the minor* that carries out that command. As such, the minor is rendered a "responsible party," so much so, that the minor is able to discharge an adult's obligation [in certain situations].

III. JEWISH EDUCATION: IT'S CRITICAL

Educating a Child to Make It Their Own

TEXT 10

THE REBBE, RABBI MENACHEM MENDEL SCHNEERSON, IBID., P. 241

דוקא דורך דעם וואס מ'גיט דעם קינד א חינוך במצוות ווערט ער א מציאות בפני עצמו און האט אן אייגענעם פארבונד מיט דער מצוה (כנזכר לעיל אז דער קטן אליין ווערט אנגערופן א מחויב בדבר).

The only way to ensure that a Jewish child assumes their own identity and creates a personal connection with the *mitzvot* is if they are properly educated about them. This is in line with our discussion here, namely that the mitzvah of education renders the minor a responsible party.

More on the Importance of Jewish Education

TEXT 11

THE REBBE, RABBI MENACHEM MENDEL SCHNEERSON,
TORAT MENACHEM 5744:3, P. 1434

לדאבוננו, ישנם הורים שדואגים לכל צרכיו הגשמיים של הילד – אכילה ושתיה, לבוש, צעצועים וכיוצא בזה, ואילו בנוגע לשאר הענינים, החל מהענין הכי עיקרי, שהילד יגדל להיות "אדם" הראוי לשמו, המתנהג בדרך הישרה – אינם שמים לב לכך, מפני טרדות הפרנסה וכיוצא בזה, וסומכים על כך שכל שאר הענינים יקבל הילד ב"בית הספר".

ועל כך מדגישה התורה – "תורת אמת" ו"תורת חיים" – שעיקר האחריות והדאגה לחינוך הילד מוטלת על ההורים, ואילו "בית הספר" אינו אלא בתור "שליח" שלהם, ומכיון שכן, הרי גם כאשר שולחים את הילד ל"בית ספר" – נשארת האחריות על כתפיהם של ההורים.

בודאי זקוקים גם לחינוך בבית הספר . . . אבל ביחד עם זה – אין להסתפק במה שנותנים לילד בבית הספה, אלא ההורים מצדם צריכים לתת לילד את כל מה שבכחם לתת.

Sadly, many parents worry about their children's material concerns—food, clothing, toys, and the like—whereas, when it comes to other things, such as the all-important concern that their child grow up as a proper *mentsh*, they don't pay as much attention. Whether it is because of financial concerns or other matters, they rely on the fact that their child will get everything they need from school.

It is regarding such an attitude that the Torah stresses that the party primarily responsible for a child's education is his or her parents. The school is only the parents' agent in this mission. As such, even after the parents send their child off to school, the responsibility remains on the parents' shoulders.

Of course, the children need schooling. However, it is not enough; the parents must do whatever they can to educate their own children.

TEXT 12

THE REBBE, RABBI MENACHEM MENDEL SCHNEERSON,
TORAT MENACHEM 5716:2 (16), PP. 205–206

בכדי שהבנים, וכן התלמידים (הנקראים בנים, כדרשת הספרי), יהיו כדבעי – מוכרח להיות עמל, מוכרחים להתייגע על זה.

מי שיש לו בנים ממושמעים, מי שיש לו השפעה על תלמידיו עד שכאשר אומר להם מלה אחת הרי זה מספיק כבר עבורם – אל לו לחשוב שבזה יצא ידי חובה בעבודתו. גם באופן כזה – בהכרח להתייגע על חינוכם. "עמלנו" – עמל כזה, שהתורה אומרת עליו שנחשב לעמל ("דאס הייסט געהארעוועט").

Educating children, or students, along the proper path requires a lot of hard work.

Even if one has dutiful children or students for whom one word is enough to get them into line, the educator must not make the mistake of thinking that their job is done. Even in such situations, the educator must invest and work hard at their job, to the degree that the Torah can label it "hard work."

TEXT 13

THE REBBE, RABBI MENACHEM MENDEL SCHNEERSON,
TORAT MENACHEM 5717:2 (19), P. 65

עיקר התמסרותם של ההורים צריך להיות בנוגע לחינוך הילדים בדרך התורה והמצות, כדי להבטיח שהילדים יגדלו להיות חסידים, יראי שמים ולומדים, שעל ידי זה מביאים אושר נצחי להילדים וכן להורים.

אבל כאשר מתמסרים לקשט את הילד במלבושים יקרים, כדי שהילד שלו ילך לבוש בבגדים יפים יותר מילדיהם של השכנים, הרי, אושר כזה יכול להמשך ליום, שבוע, חודש, שנה. אבל לאחר זה, כאשר הילד יגדל, רואים שהחסירו להעניק לו את האושר האמיתי שעל ידו יהיה מאושר במשך כל ימי חייו.

Parents' primary dedication ought to be to provide their children with a robust Jewish education. Parents should be committed to raising children who are pious, G-d fearing, and students of the Torah. This will bring both parties lasting joy.

When parents decide to commit their energy to providing their child with nice clothing so that he or she can be the best-dressed kid in the neighborhood, well, such joy only lasts a day, a week, a month, or maybe even a year. But thereafter, when the child matures, it becomes obvious that he or she was deprived of true joy that could have lasted their entire life.

KEY POINTS

- There's a mitzvah to count the days between Pesach and Shavuot in anticipation of the gift that is the Torah. This is called *Sefirat ha'Omer*.
- A parent is obligated to educate, or train, their child in mitzvah observance and Torah study once the child is mature enough.
- While this obligation is incumbent upon the parents, inasmuch as the child is a critical party to the obligation, it extends over to the child as well.
- Parents must take the responsibility of giving their child a robust Jewish education seriously. It requires commitment and hard work—without relying on others to do it.

3.

Emor

Jews Don't Pray. They *Daven*.

G-d Is Not a Vending Machine

Dedicated to David and Harriet Moldau, in appreciation of their friendship and partnership with JLI and their dedication to bringing the light of Torah to communities across the globe.

PARSHAH OVERVIEW

Emor

The Torah section of *Emor* ("speak") begins with the special laws pertaining to the *Kohanim* (priests), the *Kohen Gadol* (High Priest), and the Temple service: A *Kohen* may not become ritually impure through contact with a dead body, save on the occasion of the death of a close relative. A *Kohen* may not marry a divorcée, or a woman with a promiscuous past; a *Kohen Gadol* can marry only a virgin. A *Kohen* with a physical deformity cannot serve in the Holy Temple, nor can a deformed animal be brought as an offering.

A newborn calf, lamb, or kid must be left with its mother for seven days before being eligible to be an offering; one may not slaughter an animal and its offspring on the same day.

The second part of *Emor* lists the annual Callings of Holiness—the festivals of the Jewish calendar: the weekly Shabbat; the bringing of the Passover offering on 14 Nisan; the seven-day Passover festival beginning on 15 Nisan; the bringing of the *Omer* offering from the first barley harvest on the second day of Passover, and the commencement, on that day, of the forty-nine-day counting of the *Omer*, culminating in the festival of Shavuot on the fiftieth day; a "remembrance of shofar blowing" on 1 Tishrei; a solemn fast day on 10 Tishrei; the Sukkot festival—during which we are to dwell in huts for seven days and take the four kinds—beginning on 15 Tishrei; and the immediately following holiday of the "eighth day" of Sukkot (Shemini Atzeret).

Next, the Torah discusses the lighting of the *menorah* in the Temple, and the showbread (*lechem hapanim*) placed weekly on the table there.

INTRODUCTION

Exercise

Think about a time when you prayed to G-d and you found it difficult to focus or otherwise "get into it." What specifically was challenging about it?

____

____

Now think of a time when you prayed and it "worked" in whichever way. What was enriching about it? Why did it work?

____

____

I. MUST WE PRAY?

Sefirah: *An Opportune Time for Prayer*

TEXT 1A

TALMUD, BERACHOT 4B

אָמַר רַבִּי יוֹחָנָן: אֵיזֶהוּ בֶּן הָעוֹלָם הַבָּא? זֶה הַסּוֹמֵךְ גְּאוּלָּה לִתְפִלָּה שֶׁל עַרְבִית.

Rabbi Yochanan said, "Who is assured a place in the World to Come? One who juxtaposes the blessing of Redemption, recited after Shema, to the evening prayer."

Babylonian Talmud

A literary work of monumental proportions that draws upon the legal, spiritual, intellectual, ethical, and historical traditions of Judaism. The 37 tractates of the Babylonian Talmud contain the teachings of the Jewish sages from the period after the destruction of the 2nd Temple through the 5th century CE. It has served as the primary vehicle for the transmission of the Oral Law and the education of Jews over the centuries; it is the entry point for all subsequent legal, ethical, and theological Jewish scholarship.

TEXT 1B

STUDENTS OF RABBI YONAH OF GERONA ON RIF (RABBI ISAAC ALFASI'S COMMENTARY) ON TALMUD, BERACHOT 2B

הקדוש ברוך הוא, כשגאלנו והוציאנו ממצרים, היה להיותנו לו לעבדים, שנאמר: "כי עבדי הם אשר הוצאתי אותם מארץ מצרים". ובברכת גאל ישראל מזכיר בה החסד שעשה עמנו הבורא. והתפלה היא עבודה, כדאמרינן: "ועבדתם את ה' אלקיכם" זו היא תפלה. וכשהוא מזכיר יציאת מצרים ומתפלל - מיד מראה שכמו שהעבד שקונה אותו רבו חייב לעשות מצות רבו, כן הוא מכיר הטובה והגאולה שגאל אותו הבורא ושהוא עבדו ועובד אותו.

וכיון שמכיר שהוא עבדו מפני שגאלו ועושה רצונו ומצותיו, נמצא שבעבור זה זוכה לחיי העולם הבא.

G-d redeemed us from Egypt to be His servants, as the verse states, "For they are My servants, whom I brought out of the land of Egypt" (Leviticus 25:42). In the blessing of Redemption, we mention G-d's kindness to us, and prayer is also "service," as the Talmud states, "To love G-d, and to serve Him with all your heart—this refers to prayer" (Taanit 2a). So, when we mention the Exodus and immediately pray, we demonstrate that just as a servant is obligated to follow his master's command, so do we recognize the kindness that G-d did to us and that we are indentured in His service.

Recognizing that we are G-d's servant because He redeemed us motivates us to fulfill His *mitzvot*. In turn, we merit a portion in the World to Come.

Rabbi Yonah of Gerona
c. 1210–c. 1263

Spanish Talmudist and ethicist. A native of Gerona, Catalonia, Rabbi Yonah studied with leading figures of the Tosafist school in France, thus combining Ashkenazic and Sefardic scholarship. He wrote biblical and Talmudic commentaries, and he is best known for his moralistic works on repentance and ethical conduct.

The Mitzvah of Prayer

TEXT 2A

MAIMONIDES, *MISHNEH TORAH,* LAWS OF PRAYER 1:1

מצות עשה להתפלל בכל יום, שנאמר: "ועבדתם את ה' אלקיכם".

It is a positive Torah commandment to pray every day, as the verse states, "You shall serve G-d" (Exodus 23:25).

Rabbi Moshe ben Maimon (Maimonides, Rambam) 1135–1204

Halachist, philosopher, author, and physician. Maimonides was born in Córdoba, Spain. After the conquest of Córdoba by the Almohads, he fled Spain and eventually settled in Cairo, Egypt. There, he became the leader of the Jewish community and served as court physician to the vizier of Egypt. He is most noted for authoring the *Mishneh Torah*, an encyclopedic arrangement of Jewish law; and for his philosophical work, *Guide for the Perplexed*. His rulings on Jewish law are integral to the formation of Halachic consensus.

TEXT 2B

RABBI AHARON HALEVI OF BARCELONA, *SEFER HACHINUCH* 433

מצות תפילה . . . שהמצוה היא להתפלל ולזעוק לפני הא-ל ברוך הוא בעת הצרה.

The mitzvah of prayer is . . . to pray and call out to G-d at any time of distress.

Rabbi Aharon Halevi of Barcelona (Re'ah) 1235–1290

Born in Gerona, Spain. Rabbi, Talmudist, and authority on Jewish law. Rabbi Aharon studied under Nachmanides and under his father, Rabbi Yosef Halevi, and corresponded with the leading Talmudic scholars of his generation. His explanations on the Rashba's Halachic code, *Torat Habayit*, entitled *Bedek Habayit*, are integral in the formation of Jewish law. Rabbi Aharon was considered by some to be the anonymous author of *Sefer Hachinuch*, a compendium of the 613 commandments.

TEXT 3

DEUTERONOMY 11:13

וְהָיָה אִם שָׁמֹעַ תִּשְׁמְעוּ אֶל מִצְוֹתַי אֲשֶׁר אָנֹכִי מְצַוֶּה אֶתְכֶם הַיּוֹם, לְאַהֲבָה אֶת ה' אֱלֹקֵיכֶם וּלְעָבְדוֹ בְּכָל לְבַבְכֶם וּבְכָל נַפְשְׁכֶם.

And it will be, if you hearken to My commandments that I command you this day to love your G-d, and to serve Him with all your heart and with all your soul.

No Mitzvah at All

TEXT 4A

NACHMANIDES, GLOSSES TO MAIMONIDES'S *SEFER HAMITZVOT*, MITZVAH 5

אלא ודאי כל ענין התפלה אינו חובה כלל, אבל הוא ממדת חסד הבורא יתברך עלינו, ששומע ועונה בכל קראנו אליו.

The entire notion of prayer isn't compulsory at all. Rather, it is a great kindness that G-d has afforded us, that He listens and responds any time we call out to Him.

Rabbi Moshe ben Nachman (Nachmanides, Ramban)
1194–1270

Scholar, philosopher, author, and physician. Nachmanides was born in Spain and served as leader of Iberian Jewry. In 1263, he was summoned by King James of Aragon to a public disputation with Pablo Cristiani, a Jewish apostate. Though Nachmanides was the clear victor of the debate, he had to flee Spain because of the resulting persecution. He moved to Israel and helped reestablish communal life in Jerusalem. He authored a classic commentary on the Pentateuch and a commentary on the Talmud.

TEXT 4B

NACHMANIDES, IBID.

ועיקר הכתוב "ולעבדו בכל לבבכם" - מצות עשה שתהיה כל עבודתנו לא-ל יתעלה בכל לבבנו, כלומר, בכוונה רצויה שלימה לשמו ובאין הרהור רע, לא שנעשה המצות בלי כונה או על הספק אולי יש בהם תועלת, כענין "ואהבת את ה' אלקיך בכל לבבך ובכל נפשך ובכל מאדך", שהמצוה היא לאהוב את ה' בכל לב ולב, ושנסתכן באהבתו בנפשנו ובממוננו.

The primary message of the verse, "Serve G-d with all your heart," is to hand down a positive commandment that all our G-dly service should be with a full heart, namely with proper intention for His name and without any negative thoughts. We should never do any of the *mitzvot* without intention or doubting whether or not they have any purpose. This is in the spirit of the verse, "And you shall love G-d with all your soul and all your might" (Deuteronomy 6:5), namely there is a mitzvah to love G-d with a full heart, so much so that we're willing to risk our property and our lives for this love.

TEXT 5A

RABBI YOSEF ALBO, *SEFER HA'IKARIM* 4:16

והוא דבר ראוי ומחוייב על כל מאמין בהשגחה שיאמין שהתפלה תועיל לו להצילו מרעתו, כי מי שלא יתפלל לה' בעת צרתו – הנה הוא אם מפני שלא יאמין בהשגחה, ואם שיאמין בה אבל יספק ביכולת ה' על הצלתו, ושתיהן כפירה.

It's only appropriate that anyone who believes in providence must believe that prayer will help them and save them from misfortune. If one does not pray in a time of trouble, it is either because they don't believe in providence, or because though they do believe in providence, they doubt G-d's ability to save them—both of which are forms of disbelief.

Rabbi Yosef Albo
c. 1380–1444

Spanish rabbi and philosopher. A student of Rabbi Chasdai Crescas, Albo is renowned for his philosophical work *Sefer Ha'ikarim* (*Book of Fundamentals*). The work stresses three fundamental aspects of Jewish belief: the existence of G-d, Torah from Sinai, and reward and punishment.

TEXT 5B

RABBI MENACHEM MENDEL OF LUBAVITCH, *DERECH MITZVOTECHA, SHORESH MITZVAT HATEFILAH* 115A

וזהו משרשי האמונה, והוא לפי שעל ידי זה ידע ויבין שה' יתברך הוא לבדו המנהיג עולמו ומשגיח בכל פרטי בריותיו, וכי לו לבדו היכולת להושיע כו'.

Prayer is one of the foundations of our belief because through prayer, a person comes to know and understand that G-d alone runs the world and supervises every detail of His creatures, and that He alone has the ability to deliver salvation.

Rabbi Menachem Mendel of Lubavitch (*Tzemach Tzedek*)
1789–1866

Chasidic rebbe and noted author. The *Tzemach Tzedek* was the third leader of the Chabad Chasidic movement and a noted authority on Jewish law. His numerous works include Halachic responsa, Chasidic discourses, and kabbalistic writings. Active in the communal affairs of Russian Jewry, he worked to alleviate the plight of the cantonists, Jewish children kidnapped to serve in the czar's army. He passed away in Lubavitch, leaving seven sons and two daughters.

II. AN EMOTIONAL EXPERIENCE

Defining Prayer: A Mitzvah for the Heart

TEXT 6

TALMUD, TAANIT 2A

דתניא: "לאהבה את ה' אלקיכם ולעבדו בכל לבבכם", איזו היא עבודה שהיא בלב? הוי אומר זו תפילה.

It was taught regarding the verse, "To love G-d and to serve Him with all your heart" (Deuteronomy 11:13). Which is the service of G-d that is performed in the heart? You must say that this is referring to prayer.

TEXT 7

MAIMONIDES, *MISHNEH TORAH*, LAWS OF PRAYER 1:2

חיוב מצוה זו כך הוא: שיהא אדם מתחנן ומתפלל בכל יום ומגיד שבחו של הקדוש ברוך הוא, ואחר כך שואל צרכיו שהוא צריך להם בבקשה ובתחינה, ואחר כך נותן שבח והודיה לה' על הטובה שהשפיע לו, כל אחד לפי כוחו.

This commandment obligates each person to offer supplication and prayer every day and utter praises of the Holy One, blessed be He; then petition for all his needs with requests and supplications; and finally, give praise and thanks to G-d for the goodness that He has bestowed upon him, each one according to his own ability.

TEXT 8

THE REBBE, RABBI MENACHEM MENDEL SCHNEERSON, *LIKUTEI SICHOT* 22, P. 117

מצות התפלה איז מיוחד בזה, אז אף על פי אז תפלה מוז זיין בדיבור דוקא, איז אבער די "מעשה" המצוה פון תפלה – "שיהא אדם מתחנן ומתפלל בכל יום": דער תוכן פון "מתחנן" איז עבודה ורגש בלב האדם – ניט עשיה אדער דיבור.

און אף על פי אז בכמה מצות איז דער דין אז די מצות של תורה "צריכות כוונה לצאת ידי חובתו בעשיית אותה מצוה", און בשעת עס פעלט די כוונה "לא יצא ידי חובתו מן התורה" – איז עס נאר אן ענין פון כוונת המצוה, אבער ניט א חלק פון דער מצוה גופא.

בא תפלה אבער איז די חפצא פון מעשה התפלה – "מתחנן ומתפלל", כוונת הלב.

Rabbi Menachem Mendel Schneerson 1902–1994

The towering Jewish leader of the 20th century, known as "the Lubavitcher Rebbe," or simply as "the Rebbe." Born in southern Ukraine, the Rebbe escaped Nazi-occupied Europe, arriving in the U.S. in June 1941. The Rebbe inspired and guided the revival of traditional Judaism after the European devastation, impacting virtually every Jewish community the world over. The Rebbe often emphasized that the performance of just one additional good deed could usher in the era of Mashiach. The Rebbe's scholarly talks and writings have been printed in more than 200 volumes.

The mitzvah of prayer is unique from other *mitzvot*. While one must indeed verbally articulate the words of prayer, that is not the "act of the mitzvah," rather it is "to offer supplication and prayer [to G-d] every day." "Supplications" are things that are felt in a person's heart—not in action or even speech.

Now, it's true that all *mitzvot* need to be performed with intention, and if one performs a mitzvah without intention, they have not discharged their Torah obligation. Still, this is only about the intentions that must be incorporated into the mitzvah, not the actual mitzvah itself.

By contrast, when it comes to prayer, the act of the mitzvah is defined as devotion and feeling of the heart.

Preparing for Prayer

TEXT 9A

MAIMONIDES, *MISHNEH TORAH*, LAWS OF PRAYER 4:16

> כיצד היא הכוונה?
>
> שיפנה את ליבו מכל המחשבות, ויראה עצמו כאילו הוא עומד לפני השכינה. לפיכך צריך לישב מעט קודם התפילה כדי לכוון את ליבו, ואחר כך יתפלל בנחת ובתחנונים.

What is meant by [proper] intention?

One should clear his mind from all thoughts and envision himself as standing before the Divine Presence. Therefore, one must sit a short while before praying in order to focus his attention, and then pray in a pleasant and supplicatory fashion.

TEXT 9B

MISHNAH, BERACHOT 5:1

> חֲסִידִים הָרִאשׁוֹנִים הָיוּ שׁוֹהִים שָׁעָה אַחַת וּמִתְפַּלְלִים, כְּדֵי שֶׁיְּכַוְּנוּ אֶת לִבָּם לַמָּקוֹם.

The original pious ones used to wait one hour and then pray, in order to direct their hearts toward G-d.

Mishnah

The first authoritative work of Jewish law that was codified in writing. The Mishnah contains the oral traditions that were passed down from teacher to student; it supplements, clarifies, and systematizes the commandments of the Torah. Due to the continual persecution of the Jewish people, it became increasingly difficult to guarantee that these traditions would not be forgotten. Rabbi Yehudah Hanasi therefore redacted the Mishnah at the end of the 2nd century. It serves as the foundation for the Talmud.

III. THE SOUL OF JUDAISM

The Soul of Prayer

TEXT 10

FROM THE TALKS AND WRITINGS OF RABBI YOSEF YITZCHAK SCHNEERSOHN, ADAPTED BY RABBI YANKI TAUBER, WWW.CHABAD.ORG/58175

When Rabbi Schneur Zalman of Liadi, the founder of Chabad, neared his twentieth year, he decided—with the consent of his wife, Rebbetzin Sterna—to travel to a center of Torah learning and service of G-d.

At that time Vilna and Mezeritch were the great Jewish capitals of eastern Europe. Vilna was the seat of Rabbi Eliyahu, the famed Gaon of Vilna, and Mezeritch was the hometown of Rabbi DovBer (the "Maggid"), leader of the Chasidic movement.

Related Rabbi Schneur Zalman, "I debated as to where I should go. I knew that in Vilna one was taught how to study, and that in Mezeritch one could learn how to pray. To study I was somewhat able, but of prayer I knew very little. So I went to Mezeritch.

"The Almighty blessed me with making the right choice. I became a devoted disciple of our Rebbe's and, upon my return to Vitebsk, I guided my students in the teachings of Chassidism, which were well received by them."

Rabbi Yosef Yitzchak Schneersohn (Rayatz, Frierdiker Rebbe, Previous Rebbe)
1880–1950

Chasidic rebbe, prolific writer, and Jewish activist. Rabbi Yosef Yitzchak, the sixth leader of the Chabad movement, actively promoted Jewish religious practice in Soviet Russia and was arrested for these activities. After his release from prison and exile, he settled in Warsaw, Poland, from where he fled Nazi occupation and arrived in New York in 1940. Settling in Brooklyn, Rabbi Schneersohn worked to revitalize American Jewish life. His son-in-law Rabbi Menachem Mendel Schneerson succeeded him as the leader of the Chabad movement.

TEXT 11

THE REBBE, RABBI MENACHEM MENDEL SCHNEERSON, *HAYOM YOM*, 23 IYAR

ראשית הירידה, רחמנא ליצלן, הוא העדר העבודה בתפילה, עס ווערט אלץ טרוקען און קאלט, די מצות אנשים מלומדה ווערט שוין אויך שווער, מען איילט, מען ווערט אן דעם געשמאק אין תורה, והאויר מתגשם, ומובן הדבר שאינו שייך כלל לפעול על הזולת.

The first stage in a person's spiritual decline (Heaven forbid) is a lack of effort when serving G-d in prayer. Everything becomes parched and cold. Even the routine performance of *mitzvot* becomes burdensome. One hurries [through their observance] and loses a taste for Torah study. The very atmosphere becomes more materially oriented. And it goes without saying that a person in such a state cannot positively influence others at all.

Hayom Yom

In 1942, Rabbi Yosef Yitzchak Schneersohn, the 6th rebbe of Chabad, gave his son-in-law, the future Rebbe, the task of compiling an anthology of Chasidic aphorisms and customs arranged according to the days of the year. In describing the completed product, Rabbi Yosef Yitzchak wrote that it is "a book that is small in format but bursting with pearls and diamonds of the choicest quality."

TEXT 12

RABBI SHNEUR ZALMAN OF LIADI, LAWS OF TALMUD TORAH 4:5

אמרו שחסידים הראשונים היו שוהין שעה אחת שלימה בכל תפלת י"ח משלש תפילות שבכל יום, ושעה אחת שלימה קודם כל תפילה ושעה אחת שלימה אחר כל תפילה, ונמצא שוהין ט' שעות ביום.

ולא היו חוששין לביטול תורה, אף שתלמוד תורה כנגד כולם -

מפני שהיו מקשרים דעתם לאדון הכל ברוך הוא ביראה ואהבה עזה ודביקות אמיתית, עד שהיו מגיעים להתפשטות הגשמיות. ומצות הדביקות האמיתית ביראה ואהבה היא גדולה ממצות תלמוד תורה וקודמת אליה, כמו שכתוב: "ראשית חכמה יראת ה'".

Rabbi Shneur Zalman of Liadi (Alter Rebbe)
1745–1812

Chasidic rebbe, Halachic authority, and founder of the Chabad movement. The Alter Rebbe was born in Liozna, Belarus, and was among the principal students of the Magid of Mezeritch. His numerous works include the *Tanya*, an early classic containing the fundamentals of Chabad Chasidism; and *Shulchan Aruch HaRav*, an expanded and reworked code of Jewish law.

The Talmud describes how "the original pious ones used to wait one hour" for each one of the three prayers of the day, as well as spend an hour praying, and then wait another hour thereafter. It turns out that they spent nine hours engaged in prayer every day.

Why were they not concerned with the time it took away from Torah study, which is equivalent to all other *mitzvot*?

It is because when they prayed, they would connect with G-d with such a strong and authentic sense of love and fear that they would be stripped of all materialism. An authentic connection with G-d with such love and fear is an even greater mitzvah than Torah study and supersedes it, as the verse states, "The beginning of wisdom is the fear of G-d" (Psalms 111:10).

Doing "Work"

TEXT 13

THE REBBE, RABBI MENACHEM MENDEL SCHNEERSON, *LIKUTEI SICHOT* 22, P. 118

וויבאלד אז די מציאות פון תפלה ווערט געשאפן על ידי כוונת (עבודת) האדם, איז מובן, אז לכל לראש, איז דער שינוי וועלכער ווערט אין דעם "גברא" על ידי התפלה והקדמתו לזה . . .

תפלה, וואס עיקרה איז תפלת העמידה, איז וואס א איד איז עומד, שטעלט זיך כעבדא קמיה מריה פאר דעם אויבערשטן, "ויראה עצמו כאילו הוא עומד לפני השכינה", וואס דעמאלט איז ער "מתחנן ומתפלל" – ער ווערט א מציאות פון א מתפלל.

בשעת אן אדם איז "מפנה את לבו מכל המחשבות כו'" און איז מתחנן ומתפלל פאר דעם אויבערשטן, ווערט ער מיט דעם גופא נשתנה און נתעלה ממצבו הקודם, ער שטייט אין א מעמד ומצב שונה לגמרי, עס ווערט א שינוי וחידוש אין דעם גברא.

Inasmuch as the very act of prayer is created through human work, it only makes sense that the primary change occurs in the person who prays. . . .

The principal idea of prayer is the notion that one stands as a servant before their master, before G-d Himself. One ought to imagine themselves standing before G-d's presence, and then they become an "entity that prays."

When a person clears out any distracting thoughts and pours out their heart to G-d, that alone changes them from their previous standing. They are now in a higher space, a changed person.

Prayer Isn't Just One Mitzvah

TEXT 14

MISHNAH, OHALOT 1:8

מאתים וארבעים ושמונה איברים באדם . . . ושמונה עשרה חוליות בשדרה.

There are 248 limbs in the body . . . and eighteen vertebrae in the spine.

TEXT 15

RABBI SHNEUR ZALMAN OF LIADI, *LIKUTEI TORAH*, BALAK, 70D

אך החוט השדרה עצמו הנמשך בתוך החוליות אינו ממנין האברים, ועם כל זה הוא המעמיד ומקיים את כל האברים שמבריח מן הראש עד הירכיים, ועל ידו נמשך החיות מהמוחין לכל האברים, שהאברים מחוברים בצלעות . . . ומתפשט עד הרגלים, ולכן אם נפסק חוט השדרה כו'.

כמו כן הנמשל בבחינת המצות שהם רמ"ח אברים דמלכא. הנה אמרו רבותינו ז"ל: "מצות צריכות כוונה", והכוונה היינו בחינת התפלה, שהיא בחינת כוונה ופנימית להמצות, והיא עיקר המעמיד ומקיים את הרמ"ח מצות עשה. והיא כמשל החוט השדרה שהוא המעמיד ומקיים את האברים אף על פי שהוא בעצמו אינו ממנין רמ"ח אברים.

The spinal cord that runs through all the vertebrae is not on the list of limbs, and yet, it is what sustains and bridges all the limbs from the head all the way to the hips. It is what delivers life-giving energy from the brain to the rest of the body by way of the hips and thighs, . . . all the way to the feet. Heaven protect us from the consequences of the spinal cord being severed.

And so it is in the analog with the *mitzvot*, which are the 248 limbs of the King G-d. Our sages declare that "all *mitzvot* need *kavanah*" (Talmud, Berachot 13a) and that *kavanah* is prayer. Prayer is the inner *kavanah* of every other mitzvah, and it is the mainstay that supports and animates all active *mitzvot*. It is precisely like the spinal cord that sustains all other limbs while not being counted as one of the 248 limbs itself.

KEY POINTS

- *Sefirat ha'Omer* is an opportune time to focus on the topic of prayer.
- Most Halachic authorities consider prayer a biblical obligation. One minority opinion does not.
- The legal definition of prayer is articulating requests to G-d. But all sources indicate that prayer is supposed to be an emotional, heartfelt experience as well.
- These two elements are the body and soul of prayer. The soul is about bonding with G-d.
- The soul of prayer is so fundamental, it is really what underpins the entirety of Judaism. That accounts for the minority opinion above, for it is too broad to be pinned down into one mitzvah.

4.

Behar—Bechukotai

“Pull Yourself Up by Your Own Bootstraps,” They Said. It’s a Lie.

You Can’t Jump Out of Your Own Skin. Get an Objective Opinion.

Dedicated in loving memory of David Rock,
דוד שמואל בן זלמן גרשון ז"ל,
marking his yahrtzeit *on 14 Iyar.*

May the merit of the Torah study worldwide accompany his soul in the world of everlasting life and be a source of blessings to his family, with much health, happiness, nachas, *and success.*

PARSHAH OVERVIEW

Behar

On the mountain of Sinai, G-d communicates to Moses the laws of the sabbatical year. Every seventh year, all work on the land should cease, and its produce becomes free for the taking for all, human and beast.

Seven sabbatical cycles are followed by a fiftieth year—the jubilee year, on which work on the land ceases, all indentured servants are set free, and all ancestral estates in the Holy Land that have been sold revert to their original owners.

Behar also contains additional laws governing the sale of lands, and the prohibitions against fraud and usury.

Bechukotai

G-d promises that if the people of Israel will keep His commandments, they will enjoy material prosperity and dwell securely in their homeland. But He also delivers a harsh "rebuke" warning of the exile, persecution, and other evils that will befall them if they abandon their covenant with Him.

Nevertheless, "Even when they are in the land of their enemies, I will not cast them away; nor will I ever abhor them, to destroy them and to break My covenant with them, for I am the L-rd their G-d."

The *parshah* concludes with the rules on how to calculate the values of different types of pledges made to G-d, and the mitzvah of tithing produce and livestock.

INTRODUCTION

Exercise

Take a look at this picture:

Can you guess what this person is trying to do?

Why is this absurd?

____

____

I. A MAN IN DECLINE

Buying Your Way to Redemption

TEXT 1

LEVITICUS 25:47–49

מז. וְכִי תַשִּׂיג יַד גֵּר וְתוֹשָׁב עִמָּךְ וּמָךְ אָחִיךָ עִמּוֹ, וְנִמְכַּר לְגֵר תּוֹשָׁב עִמָּךְ
אוֹ לְעֵקֶר מִשְׁפַּחַת גֵּר:

מח. אַחֲרֵי נִמְכַּר גְּאֻלָּה תִּהְיֶה לּוֹ, אֶחָד מֵאֶחָיו יִגְאָלֶנּוּ:

מט. אוֹ דֹדוֹ אוֹ בֶן דֹּדוֹ יִגְאָלֶנּוּ, אוֹ מִשְּׁאֵר בְּשָׂרוֹ מִמִּשְׁפַּחְתּוֹ יִגְאָלֶנּוּ, אוֹ
הִשִּׂיגָה יָדוֹ וְנִגְאָל:

47. If a resident non-Jew gains wealth with you, and your brother becomes destitute with him and is sold to a resident non-Jew among you or to an idol of the family of a non-Jew:

48. After he is sold, he shall have redemption; one of his brothers shall redeem him.

49. Or his uncle or his cousin shall redeem him, or the closest [other] relative from his family shall redeem him; or, if he becomes able to afford it, he can be redeemed [on his own].

Story of Spiritual Decline

TEXT 2

RASHI, LEVITICUS 26:1

הפרשיות הללו נאמרו על הסדר: בתחלה הזהיר על השביעית, ואם חמד ממון ונחשד על השביעית סופו למכור מטלטליו, לכך סמך לה

Rabbi Shlomo Yitzchaki (Rashi)
1040–1105

Most noted biblical and Talmudic commentator. Born in Troyes, France, Rashi studied in the famed *yeshivot* of Mainz and Worms. His commentaries on the Pentateuch and the Talmud, which focus on the straightforward meaning of the text, appear in virtually every edition of the Talmud and Bible.

"וכי תמכרו ממכר", מה כתיב ביה? "או קנה מיד עמיתך", דבר הנקנה מיד ליד.

לא חזר בו, סוף מוכר אחוזתו.

לא חזר בו, סוף מוכר את ביתו.

לא חזר בו, סוף לוה ברבית.

כל אלו האחרונות קשות מן הראשונות.

לא חזר בו, סוף מוכר את עצמו. לא חזר בו, לא דיו לישראל אלא אפילו לנכרי.

The passages [in this whole section] are written in a meaningful order, as follows: At first, Scripture admonishes us to observe [the laws of] *shemitah*. Then, if one covets money and becomes suspect of [unlawfully doing business with produce of] *shemitah*, he will eventually [become destitute and] have to sell his personal belongings. Therefore, Scripture juxtaposes to it, "And when you make a sale [to your fellow Jew]." What is written therein? "Or make a purchase from the hand . . . " (Leviticus 25:14); something that is transferred from hand to hand.

If he still does not repent, he will eventually have to sell his inheritance (Ibid., 25:25).

If he even then does not repent, he will eventually have to sell his home.

If even then he does not repent, he will eventually have to borrow money with interest (Ibid., 25:35–38).

Now, the later the scenario in this passage, the more severe it is.

If he still does not repent, he will eventually have to sell himself [to his fellow Jew as a servant] (Ibid., 25:39–46); and [finally,] if he has still not repented, it is not enough that he had to be sold to his fellow Jew, but he will [be forced to sell himself] even to a non-Jew!

TEXT 3A

LEVITICUS 26:1

לֹא תַעֲשׂוּ לָכֶם אֱלִילִם וּפֶסֶל וּמַצֵּבָה לֹא תָקִימוּ לָכֶם, וְאֶבֶן מַשְׂכִּית לֹא תִתְּנוּ בְּאַרְצְכֶם לְהִשְׁתַּחֲוֹת עָלֶיהָ, כִּי אֲנִי ה' אֱלֹקֵיכֶם:

You shall not make idols for yourselves, nor shall you set up a statue or a monument for yourselves. And in your land you shall not place a pavement stone on which to prostrate yourselves, for I am the L-rd your G-d.

TEXT 3B

RASHI, AD LOC.

"לא תעשו לכם אלילם". כנגד זה הנמכר לנכרי, שלא יאמר: הואיל ורבי מגלה עריות, אף אני כמותו! הואיל ורבי עובד עבודה זרה, אף אני כמותו! הואיל ורבי מחלל שבת, אף אני כמותו! לכך נאמרו מקראות הללו.

This is addressed to the one who has been sold [as a servant] to a non-Jew, that he should not say, "Since my master has illicit relations, I will also be like him! Since my master worships idols, I will also be like him! Since my master desecrates the Sabbath, I will also be like him!" This is why these verses are stated here.

II. SPIRITUAL ORPHAN

When One Forgets Their Father in Heaven

TEXT 4

MALACHI 1:6

בֵּן יְכַבֵּד אָב וְעֶבֶד אֲדֹנָיו, וְאִם אָב אָנִי אַיֵּה כְבוֹדִי וְאִם אֲדוֹנִים אָנִי אַיֵּה מוֹרָאִי, אָמַר ה' צְבָאוֹת לָכֶם הַכֹּהֲנִים בּוֹזֵי שְׁמִי, וַאֲמַרְתֶּם בַּמֶּה בָזִינוּ אֶת שְׁמֶךָ:

"A son honors a father, and a slave his master. Now if I am a Father, where is My honor? And if I am a Master, where is My fear?" says the L-rd of Hosts to you, the priests, who despise My name. But you said, "How have we despised Your name?"

Malachi

Biblical book. The book of Malachi contains the prophecies delivered by Malachi in the 4th century BCE, at the beginning of the period of the Second Temple. Malachi was the last of the biblical prophets, and his prophecies include rebuke of the priests for their failures of leadership, as well as discourses on G-d's great love for the Jewish people.

TEXT 5

THE REBBE, RABBI MENACHEM MENDEL SCHNEERSON, *LIKUTEI SICHOT* 17, P. 299

על פי איז מובן דער טעם (פנימי) וואס "אביו" ווערט ניט דערמאנט דא . . . דער ענין המיתה ברוחניות – "רשעים שבחייהן קרויין מתים", אדער בדקות יותר: "מאן דנחית מדרגא . . . קארי ביה מיתה" – נעמט זיך דערפון וואס עס פעלט דער געדיינקען דעם אביו שבשמים.

We can now understand the spiritual reason why "father" isn't mentioned in the verse. . . . The verse speaks of someone who is spiritually dead, for "the wicked are called dead even while alive" (Talmud, Berachot 18b). In more abstract terms, anyone experiencing spiritual decline is considered to be experiencing a form of death. What causes this? The fact that the person forgets their Father in Heaven.

Rabbi Menachem Mendel Schneerson 1902–1994

The towering Jewish leader of the 20th century, known as "the Lubavitcher Rebbe," or simply as "the Rebbe." Born in southern Ukraine, the Rebbe escaped Nazi-occupied Europe, arriving in the U.S. in June 1941. The Rebbe inspired and guided the revival of traditional Judaism after the European devastation, impacting virtually every Jewish community the world over. The Rebbe often emphasized that the performance of just one additional good deed could usher in the era of Mashiach. The Rebbe's scholarly talks and writings have been printed in more than 200 volumes.

Forgetting the Chochmah *in the Soul*

TEXT 6A

RABBI SHNEUR ZALMAN OF LIADI, *TANYA, LIKUTEI AMARIM*, CH. 18

אֲפִלּוּ לְקַל שֶׁבַּקַּלִּים וּפוֹשְׁעֵי יִשְׂרָאֵל נִמְשָׁךְ בְּזִוּוּגָם נֶפֶשׁ דְּנֶפֶשׁ דְּמַלְכוּת דַּעֲשִׂיָּה . . . שֶׁבְּתוֹכָהּ מְלֻבֶּשֶׁת חָכְמָה דַּאֲצִילוּת, שֶׁבָּהּ מֵאִיר אוֹר אֵין סוֹף בָּרוּךְ הוּא מַמָּשׁ . . . וְנִמְצָא כִּי אֵין סוֹף בָּרוּךְ הוּא מְלֻבָּשׁ בִּבְחִינַת חָכְמָה שֶׁבְּנֶפֶשׁ הָאָדָם, יִהְיֶה מִי שֶׁיִּהְיֶה מִיִּשְׂרָאֵל . . .

הִנֵּה הַחָכְמָה הִיא מְקוֹר הַשֵּׂכֶל וְהַהֲבָנָה, וְהִיא לְמַעְלָה מֵהַבִּינָה שֶׁהוּא הֲבָנַת הַשֵּׂכֶל וְהַשָּׂגָתוֹ, וְהַחָכְמָה הִיא לְמַעְלָה מֵהַהֲבָנָה וְהַהַשָּׂגָה, וְהִיא מְקוֹר לָהֶן . . . וְלָכֵן מִתְלַבֵּשׁ בָּהּ אוֹר אֵין סוֹף בָּרוּךְ הוּא, דְּלֵית מַחֲשָׁבָה תְּפִיסָא בֵּיהּ כְּלָל.

וְלָכֵן כָּל יִשְׂרָאֵל, אֲפִלּוּ . . . עַמֵּי הָאָרֶץ, הֵם מַאֲמִינִים בַּה׳, שֶׁהָאֱמוּנָה הִיא לְמַעְלָה מִן הַדַּעַת וְהַהַשָּׂגָה.

Even the most insincere and sinful Jews possess by birthright in their soul . . . the level of *chochmah* that contains the essence of G-d Himself. It turns out that the essence of G-d is integrated within the soul of every Jew, whoever they may be. . . .

This *chochmah* serves as the source of all cognition, yet it is higher than the cognitive process that breaks down intellectual matter, for it is the source of it all. . . . This explains how it is the landing spot for the essence of G-d Himself that transcends all reason.

Thus, even the simplest Jew believes in G-d, for this faith is beyond reason.

Rabbi Shneur Zalman of Liadi (Alter Rebbe)
1745–1812

Chasidic rebbe, Halachic authority, and founder of the Chabad movement. The Alter Rebbe was born in Liozna, Belarus, and was among the principal students of the Magid of Mezeritch. His numerous works include the *Tanya*, an early classic containing the fundamentals of Chabad Chasidism; and *Shulchan Aruch HaRav*, an expanded and reworked code of Jewish law.

TEXT 6B

RABBI SHNEUR ZALMAN OF LIADI, IBID.

וְלָכֵן אֲפִלּוּ קַל שֶׁבַּקַּלִים וּפוֹשְׁעֵי יִשְׂרָאֵל מוֹסְרִים נַפְשָׁם עַל קְדֻשַּׁת ה' עַל הָרֹב, וְסוֹבְלִים עִנּוּיִים קָשִׁים שֶׁלֹּא לִכְפֹּר בַּה' אֶחָד, וְאַף אִם הֵם בּוּרִים וְעַמֵּי הָאָרֶץ וְאֵין יוֹדְעִים גְּדֻלַּת ה'.

וְגַם בַּמְּעַט שֶׁיּוֹדְעִים אֵין מִתְבּוֹנְנִים כְּלָל, וְאֵין מוֹסְרִים נַפְשָׁם מֵחֲמַת דַּעַת וְהִתְבּוֹנְנוּת בַּה' כְּלָל, אֶלָּא בְּלִי שׁוּם דַּעַת וְהִתְבּוֹנְנוּת, רַק כְּאִלּוּ הוּא דָּבָר שֶׁאִי אֶפְשָׁר כְּלָל לִכְפֹּר בַּה' אֶחָד, בְּלִי שׁוּם טַעַם וּטְעָנָה וּמַעֲנֶה כְּלָל.

וְהַיְנוּ מִשּׁוּם שֶׁה' אֶחָד מֵאִיר וּמְחַיֶּה כָּל הַנֶּפֶשׁ עַל יְדֵי הִתְלַבְּשׁוּתוֹ בִּבְחִינַת חָכְמָה שֶׁבָּהּ, שֶׁהִיא לְמַעְלָה מִן הַדַּעַת וְהַשֵּׂכֶל הַמֻּשָּׂג וּמוּבָן.

This also explains why even insincere and sinful Jews will typically give up their lives for G-d, or opt to suffer extreme pain rather than revolt against G-d, choosing to do so even though they are completely ignorant of anything about G-d's greatness.

Even the little they do know, they don't really process; their tremendous sacrifice is not due to any great awareness about G-d's greatness, rather it is entirely beyond reason. It's as if it is impossible to revolt against G-d, without any sort of explanation or negotiation.

The explanation for this is because the Oneness of G-d energizes and animates the soul by integrating into the *chochmah* that is higher than reason and cognition.

TEXT 6C

PRESIDENT OF ISRAEL MOSHE KATSAV
QUOTED IN JUDEA AND RUTH PEARL (EDS.), *I AM JEWISH: PERSONAL REFLECTIONS INSPIRED BY THE LAST WORDS OF DANIEL PEARL*
(WOODSTOCK ,VT.: JEWISH LIGHTS PUBLISHING, 2004), P. 67

The late Daniel Pearl, of blessed memory, by stating "I am a Jew" to his terrorist captors before being murdered, proclaimed his affiliation to a religious and national entity and his being part of Jewish history. This declaration encompasses a way of life, beliefs, and views. To be a Jew means an outlook on worldwide issues, founded on Jewish principles based on the Bible.

Every Jew feels a spiritual bond and an emotional attachment to Judaism even if, in the era of globalization, he hardly knows the basic concepts of Judaism; even if in his bookcase there are no books dealing with the Jewish faith, the Jewish People, or Jewish culture and history.

From the video of his beheading:

My name is Daniel Pearl. I'm a Jewish American from Encino, California, USA. I come from, uh, on my father's side the family is Zionist. My father's Jewish, my mother's Jewish, I'm Jewish. My family follows Judaism. We've made numerous family visits to Israel.

TEXT 7

RABBI SHNEUR ZALMAN OF LIADI, *TANYA, LIKUTEI AMARIM,* CH. 19

הָרְשָׁעִים וּפוֹשְׁעֵי יִשְׂרָאֵל קֹדֶם שֶׁבָּאוּ לִידֵי נִסָּיוֹן לְקַדֵּשׁ ה', כִּי בְּחִינַת
הַחָכְמָה שֶׁבַּנֶּפֶשׁ הָאֱלֹקִית עִם נִיצוֹץ אֱלֹקוּת מֵאוֹר אֵין סוֹף בָּרוּךְ הוּא
הַמְלֻבָּשׁ בָּהּ הֵם בִּבְחִינַת גָלוּת בְּגוּפָם, בַּנֶּפֶשׁ הַבַּהֲמִית מִצַּד הַקְלִפָּה . . .
הַמוֹלֶכֶת וּמוֹשֶׁלֶת בְּגוּפָם.

Before they are faced with the ultimatum of giving their life for G-d, the *chochmah* in the soul of sinful Jews along with the G-dly spark invested in it are in virtual captivity. The body and animal soul . . . are the ones who control their body.

TEXT 8

RABBI SHNEUR ZALMAN OF LIADI, IBID., CH. 24

דַאֲפִלּוּ אִשָּׁה הַמְנָאֶפֶת, שֶׁדַעְתָּהּ קַלָּה, הָיְתָה מוֹשֶׁלֶת בְּרוּחַ תַּאֲוָתָהּ
לוּלֵי רוּחַ שְׁטוּת שֶׁבָּהּ, הַמְכַסֶּה וּמַסְתִּיר וּמַעְלִים אֶת הָאַהֲבָה מְסֻתֶּרֶת
שֶׁבְּנַפְשָׁהּ הָאֱלֹקִית לְדָבְקָה בֶּאֱמוּנַת ה' וְיִחוּדוֹ וְאַחְדוּתוֹ, וְלֹא לִפָּרֵד
חַס וְשָׁלוֹם מֵאַחְדוּתוֹ . . . אֲבָל בֶּאֱמֶת לַאֲמִתּוֹ, אֲפִלּוּ עֲבֵרָה קַלָּה - הֲרֵי
הָעוֹבְרָהּ עוֹבֵר עַל רָצוֹן הָעֶלְיוֹן בָּרוּךְ הוּא, וְהוּא בְּתַכְלִית הַפֵּרוּד מִיִּחוּדוֹ
וְאַחְדוּתוֹ יִתְבָּרֵךְ.

Even an adulterous women who is obviously out of her senses would control her impulses if not for the "spirit of folly" that conceals the innate love within the G-dly soul that yearns to be close with G-d and never be ripped apart from His Oneness. . . . The truth is, even the slightest sin tears one entirely apart from the oneness and exclusiveness of G-d.

TEXT 9

RABBI SHNEUR ZALMAN OF LIADI, IBID., CH. 3

בְּנֶפֶשׁ הָאָדָם שֶׁנֶּחֱלֶקֶת לִשְׁתַּיִם - שֵׂכֶל וּמִדּוֹת. הַשֵּׂכֶל כּוֹלֵל חָכְמָה בִּינָה וָדַעַת, וְהַמִּדּוֹת הֵן אַהֲבַת ה׳ וּפַחְדּוֹ וְיִרְאָתוֹ וּלְפָאֲרוֹ כוּ׳. וְחָכְמָה בִּינָה וָדַעַת נִקְרְאוּ אִמּוֹת וּמָקוֹר לַמִּדּוֹת, כִּי הַמִּדּוֹת הֵן תּוֹלְדוֹת חָכְמָה בִּינָה וָדַעַת.

וּבֵאוּר הָעִנְיָן, כִּי הִנֵּה הַשֵּׂכֶל שֶׁבַּנֶּפֶשׁ הַמַּשְׂכֶּלֶת שֶׁהוּא הַמַּשְׂכִּיל כָּל דָּבָר, נִקְרָא בְּשֵׁם חָכְמָה, כֹּ״חַ מַ״ה. וּכְשֶׁמּוֹצִיא כֹּחוֹ אֶל הַפּוֹעַל, שֶׁמִּתְבּוֹנֵן בְּשִׂכְלוֹ לְהָבִין דָּבָר לַאֲשׁוּרוֹ וּלְעָמְקוֹ מִתּוֹךְ אֵיזֶה דְבַר חָכְמָה הַמְּשֻׂכָּל בְּשִׂכְלוֹ, נִקְרָא בִּינָה. וְהֵן הֵם אָב וָאֵם הַמּוֹלִידוֹת אַהֲבַת ה׳ וְיִרְאָתוֹ וּפַחְדּוֹ.

The human soul is divided into two broad categories, cognition and emotion. Cognition subdivides into three capacities of creativity (*chochmah*), processing (*binah*), and application (*daat*). Emotions subdivide into loving G-d and fearing G-d. The three cognitive capacities are called the "mother," i.e., the source of all emotion, for emotions are born out of a cognitive process.

To explain: The cognitive capacity of the rational soul that is able to perceive everything is called *chochmah*. This Hebrew word is a portmanteau of the two words "*ko'ach mah*—an abstract, unknown capacity." When this abstract potential is realized, namely when the person processes the creative flash to try and understand it properly and unpack its full depth, it is called *binah*. These two steps are the mother and father who collectively give birth to the emotions of love and fear of G-d.

III. NOMINATE A MENTOR

You Can't Redeem Yourself

TEXT 10

TALMUD, BERACHOT 5B

אָמְרִי: אֵין חָבוּשׁ מַתִּיר עַצְמוֹ מִבֵּית הָאֲסוּרִים.

They say, "A prisoner cannot free himself from prison."

Babylonian Talmud

A literary work of monumental proportions that draws upon the legal, spiritual, intellectual, ethical, and historical traditions of Judaism. The 37 tractates of the Babylonian Talmud contain the teachings of the Jewish sages from the period after the destruction of the 2nd Temple through the 5th century CE. It has served as the primary vehicle for the transmission of the Oral Law and the education of Jews over the centuries; it is the entry point for all subsequent legal, ethical, and theological Jewish scholarship.

TEXT 11

THE REBBE, RABBI MENACHEM MENDEL SCHNEERSON, *LIKUTEI SICHOT* 17, P. 301

וויבאלד אז בחינת הזכרון . . . פון דעם נמכר לנכרי איז בבחינת שינה, ביז ער איז כאילו געווארן אויס בעל הבית אויף זיך . . . אין אזא מצב איז פאר אים ניט מעגלעך צו זיך אליין גואל זיין, ווי דער כלל: "אין חבוש מתיר עצמו מבית האסורים";

זיין גאולה מוז קומען בדרך אתערותא דלעילא (העכער פון זיין מצב), דורך דעם וואס אנדערע (וואס זיינען ניט משועבד צו הנזכר לעיל) זיינען אים גואל.

און דערפאר שטייט צום עלעם ערשטן דער ענין פון גאולת קרובים – די אתערותא דלעילא צו ארויסשלעפן אים פון זיין שפל המצב.

For a Jew who has been "sold" into the ownership of a non-Jew, the memory of his Father in Heaven is completely forgotten, so much so that it's as if he no longer has any control over himself. . . . In such a situation, it's impossible for the slave to redeem himself, as per the rule, "A prisoner cannot free himself from prison."

His redemption must come through outside intervention, from someone in a position above his station who is not subject to the same servitude.

That is why the first option in the verse is for the relative to redeem him, namely someone from above pulling him out of his desperate situation.

Get a Mentor

TEXT 12

THE REBBE, RABBI MENACHEM MENDEL SCHNEERSON,
TORAT MENACHEM 5747:1, P. 208

גם אדם שהולך בדרך הישר, הרי, בודאי ניתן למצוא כמה וכמה ענינים שבהם יכול להוסיף עוד יותר.

אמנם, מכיון ש"אדם קרוב אצל עצמו", אינו יכול לסמוך על עצמו ולהיות בטוח שהנהגתו היא כדבעי.

ולכן, העצה לזה - "עשה לך רב", למנות לו מישהו שגדול ממנו, שישאל ויברר אצלו בנוגע לכל עניניו, הן בנוגע לענינים ד"סור מרע" והן בנוגע לענינים ד"עשה טוב".

Even someone who is completely upright, there are certainly matters in which they can improve.

However, inasmuch as everyone loves themselves, a person cannot rely on themselves to be entirely certain that they are behaving in an appropriate manner.

The solution for this problem is, as the Mishnah states, "Appoint a mentor for yourself" (Mishnah, Avot 1:6). Everyone should nominate someone greater than themselves with whom to ask and clarify all their personal affairs, be it in their efforts to abstain from negativity or proactively doing good things.

It's for Everyone—You Included

TEXT 13

THE REBBE, RABBI MENACHEM MENDEL SCHNEERSON, *LIKUTEI SICHOT* 29, P. 247

ויש להוסיף, שגם מי שהוא גדול בתורה וביראת שמים כו', שקשה לו למצוא מי שגדול ממנו – הרי "אף על פי שלא ימצא חכם גדול כמוהו, יעשה משלמטה הימנו, כי אין אדם רואה בעניני עצמו העצה הצריכה לו כמו שיראה זולתו, וזהו עשה לך רב, אף שאינו ראוי".

וכמפורש שבכגון דא יש צורך בענין של עשיה, "עשה לך רב", אשה, "לשון עשיה יאמר על דבר שצריך לטרוח ולעשות על ידו", עד לעשיה מלשון כפיה.

We should add that even [in the case of] an advanced pious Torah scholar who has trouble finding someone greater than him, then, as the Me'iri suggests, "Even if one cannot find a scholar of their own stature, they should nominate someone *inferior*, for people are unable to see the solution they need most like someone else can. Accordingly, the Mishnah's directive, 'Appoint a mentor for yourself,' means *even if they are unworthy*."

It is explicitly stated with regard to such situations that an element of coercion is necessary. The word "appoint" here connotes an active effort that requires exertion, investment, and sometimes even a little force.

Ask Me Anything

TEXT 14

THE REBBE, RABBI MENACHEM MENDEL SCHNEERSON,
TORAT MENACHEM 5747:1, P. 212

יש צורך, איפוא, להבהיר גם ענין זה, שכן, גם אם מפרשי המשנה אינם מבהירים זאת, הרי, ידע איניש בנפשיה שגם לאחרי שעושה לו רב עומד ומתלבט אם לשאול אצל הרב אודות ענין פלוני, או לדחות את השאלה וכו'.

ולכן, מצוה גדולה מדרכי המוסר להדגיש את הצורך לשאול אצל הרב בנוגע לכל עניניו, ואדרבה: דין קדימה – לשאלה אודות הענינים שמונח אצלו שהנהגתו באופן של עקמימות, או באופן גרוע מזה כו', וכן בנוגע לענינים שמסופק בהם, או בנוגע לענינים ששמע מפלוני שאין זה דבר הרצוי, או אפילו אם הבחין אצלו איזו תנועה של הסתייגות ("יענער האט א קרים געטאן מיטן נאז").

We ought to bring up something that even though the Mishnaic commentators may not bring it up, we all know it: even after nominating a mentor, we oftentimes question whether we must bring up every specific thing, or perhaps the question can wait.

And so, a great ethical principle teaches us how critical it is to ask the mentor about everything. In fact, precedence should be given to those matters about which you're fairly certain you're not behaving appropriately, or worse yet; then to matters about which you're doubtful, or things you have heard from others are not up to snuff ("someone turned up their nose").

TEXT 15

THE REBBE, RABBI MENACHEM MENDEL SCHNEERSON, *LIKUTEI SICHOT* 29, P. 248

ומה גם שעצם הידיעה שמזמן לזמן יצטרך לתת "דין וחשבון" לבשר ודם, תפעל אצלו להיטיב את הנהגתו, ולהוסיף בכל עניני טוב וקדושה.

The very knowledge that one will occasionally be held accountable to another human being will automatically improve behavior and motivate them to increase all positive, holy activity.

KEY POINTS

» The story of a slave seeking redemption in our *parshah* is also the story of a person in spiritual decline.

» The cause of this spiritual decline is forgetting one's Father in Heaven—G-d.

» Every Jew possesses an innate and suprarational commitment to G-d deep in their soul. The only way it can be "forgotten" is when it is repeatedly quashed by neglect or overindulgence in materialism.

» Regardless, this innate commitment will eventually come out.

» As subjective beings inherently incapable of making honest assessments and decisions about and for ourselves, *every person* must appoint a mentor for themselves.

5.
Bamidbar

Leadership Lessons: Personal, Local, and Global

A Multifaceted Discussion on Leadership

Dedicated to Neil and Sarah Rock, on the occasion of Neil's birthday.

May they go from strength to strength and enjoy good health, happiness, nachas *from their loved ones, and success in all of their endeavors.*

PARSHAH OVERVIEW

Bamidbar

In the Sinai Desert, G-d says to conduct a census of the twelve tribes of Israel. Moses counts 603,550 men of draftable age (twenty to sixty years); the tribe of Levi, numbering 22,300 males age one month and older, is counted separately. The Levites are to serve in the Sanctuary, replacing the firstborn, whose number they approximated, and who were disqualified when they participated in the worshipping of the Golden Calf. The 273 firstborn who lacked a Levite to replace them had to pay a five-shekel "ransom" to redeem themselves.

Each time the people break camp, the three Levite clans dismantle and transport the Sanctuary, and reassemble it at the center of the next encampment. They then erect their own tents around it: the Kehat family, who carries the Sanctuary's vessels—the ark, the *menorah*, etc., in their specially designed coverings—on their shoulders, camp to its south; the Gershonites, in charge of its tapestries and roof coverings, to its west; and the families of Merari, who transport its wall panels and pillars, to its north. Before the Sanctuary's entranceway, to its east, are the tents of Moses, Aaron, and Aaron's sons.

Beyond the Levite circle, the twelve tribes camp in four groups of three tribes each. To the east are Judah (pop. 74,600), Issachar (54,400), and Zebulun (57,400); to the south, Reuben (46,500), Simeon (59,300), and Gad (45,650); to the west, Ephraim (40,500), Manasseh (32,200), and Benjamin (35,400); and to the north, Dan (62,700), Asher (41,500), and Naphtali (53,400). This formation is kept also while traveling, each tribe with its own *nasi* (prince or leader) and its own flag with its tribal color and emblem.

I. BUY LOCAL

The Princes Introduced

TEXT 1A

NUMBERS 1:2–4

> שְׂאוּ אֶת רֹאשׁ כָּל עֲדַת בְּנֵי יִשְׂרָאֵל . . . וְאִתְּכֶם יִהְיוּ אִישׁ אִישׁ לַמַּטֶּה,
> אִישׁ רֹאשׁ לְבֵית אֲבֹתָיו הוּא.

Take the sum of the entire congregation of the Children of Israel. . . . With you there shall be one man from each tribe, the one who is head of his father's house.

TEXT 1B

NUMBERS 1:16

> אֵלֶּה קְרוּאֵי הָעֵדָה נְשִׂיאֵי מַטּוֹת אֲבוֹתָם.

These people were summoned by the nation, the princes of their paternal tribes.

Locally Selected

TEXT 2

RABBI YONATAN EYBESCHUTZ, *TIFERET YEHONASAN*, NUMBERS 1:16

נראה לפרש דלא נבחרו מפי משה כמו שהיה ראוי, כמו שנאמר: "ואתה תחזה".

אלא דאם כן יאמרו ישראל: מה אהני לן הנשיאים? המה יסכימו עם משה ודאי בכל דבר.

ולכך אמר "קרואי העדה", כי העדה נתרצו בהם.

G-d instructed Moses, "And you should choose teachers and judges" (Exodus 18:21). Nevertheless, Moses did not select the princes, though that would have been appropriate.

This was so the people would not say, "How will these leaders benefit us? They will certainly side with Moses on every matter."

Thus, the Torah describes them as "summoned by the nation" (Numbers 1:16) for the nation chose them, not Moses.

Rabbi Yonatan Eybeschutz
1690–1764

Talmudist, authority on Jewish law, and kabbalist. Recognized during his youth as a prodigy in Talmud, Rabbi Eybeschutz was appointed rabbinical magistrate of Prague, and later rabbi of Metz. In 1750, he was elected rabbi of Altona, Hamburg, and Wandsbek. He was surrounded by controversy after Rabbi Yaakov Emden accused him of Sabbatean sympathies. 30 of his works were published, including *Urim Vetumim; Kereti Upeleti; Sar Haalef* on the Code of Jewish Law; and *Ye'arot Devash,* a collection of his sermons.

The Burden of Leadership

TEXT 3A

RABBI SHLOMO EFRAIM OF LUNTSHITZ, *KELI YAKAR*, NUMBERS 1:4

מדקאמר "איש איש למטה", מה חזר ואמר "איש ראש לבית אבותיו הוא"?

וקרוב לומר . . . שלא היה מחניף לשבטו שנקראו עמו, אלא היה דן אותם . . . כאחד מן שאר שבטים . . .

לכל השבט היה כאיש גבורתו לנהוג עליהם נשיאתו ברמה. ולא זו לכל השבט הרחוקים קצת ממנו, אלא אפילו היה ראש לבית אבותיו. הקרובים אליו ביותר, גם להם היה לראש – לנהוג נשיאות עליהם.

If the passage states, "one man for each tribe," is it not redundant to tell us that each was "head of his father's house" (Numbers 1:4)?

This tells us that . . . the princes did not extend preferential treatment to their tribesmen, rather they ruled over them . . . as they would over any other tribe. . . .

Moreover, they were not just firm with distant tribal members who they barely knew but also with their father's household—their closest relatives.

Rabbi Shlomo Efraim of Luntshitz
1550–1619

After studying in the yeshiva of the Maharshal, Rabbi Shlomo Efraim gained a reputation as a distinguished preacher and scholar. He traveled far and wide to deliver his fiery sermons, which were collected and published. He is primarily known today for his work *Keli Yakar* and for his commentary on the Pentateuch, which was subsequently printed in many editions of the Bible.

Leadership Qualities

TEXT 3B

RABBI NAFTALI TZVI YEHUDAH BERLIN, *HAAMEK DAVAR*, NUMBERS 1:16

דהנשיאים היו כבר בהסכמת השבט שהוא ראוי להיות להם לראש, וכאן הקדוש ברוך הוא הסכים על ידם ומנה אותם בדבר ה'. . .

ולמדנו מזה שגם עדת ישראל לא בחרו בראש מצד עשרו והנהגת המשרה בטוב לבד, כי אם שהיו גם כן מצויינים בתורה ויראת ה' עד שראויים היו להיות ראשים, ולעמוד לפני ה' בראש השבט.

The tribes had already chosen their leaders. At this point, G-d endorsed their choices and ratified the leaders as Divine appointees. . . .

This tells us that the leaders were not chosen solely on account of their wealth and leadership qualities. They were also chosen for their brilliant Torah scholarship and their fear of Heaven. They were worthy of standing before G-d at the helm of their respective tribes.

Rabbi Naftali Tzvi Yehudah Berlin (Netziv) 1816–1893

Head of the Volozhin yeshiva, Volozhin, Russia. Rabbi Berlin was born in Mir, Russia. He applied himself to his studies and was renowned for his extraordinary diligence. He is recognized for being one of the greatest scholars of his time. In 1854, he became the head of the yeshiva, one of the largest institutions of its kind, which he led for nearly 40 years. He authored several works, including a commentary on the Talmud, and Halachic responses.

Their First Leadership Role

RASHI, NUMBERS 7:2

> שהיו שוטרים עליהם במצרים והיו מוכים עליהם.

They were the Jewish overseers in Egypt who were beaten for the sake of the Jewish slaves that they oversaw.

Rabbi Shlomo Yitzchaki (Rashi)
1040–1105

Most noted biblical and Talmudic commentator. Born in Troyes, France, Rashi studied in the famed *yeshivot* of Mainz and Worms. His commentaries on the Pentateuch and the Talmud, which focus on the straightforward meaning of the text, appear in virtually every edition of the Talmud and Bible.

The New Introduction

TEXT 5

NUMBERS 1:17

> וַיִּקַּח מֹשֶׁה וְאַהֲרֹן אֵת הָאֲנָשִׁים הָאֵלֶּה אֲשֶׁר נִקְּבוּ בְּשֵׁמוֹת.

Thus, Moses and Aaron took these men who were indicated by names.

II. IDENTIFY AND CORROBORATE

Pedigree

TEXT 6A

NUMBERS 1:18

> וְאֵת כָּל הָעֵדָה הִקְהִילוּ בְּאֶחָד לַחֹדֶשׁ הַשֵּׁנִי, וַיִּתְיַלְדוּ עַל מִשְׁפְּחֹתָם לְבֵית אֲבֹתָם.

The entire nation assembled on the first day of the second month and declared their pedigrees according to their families and according to their fathers' houses.

TEXT 6B

RASHI, AD LOC.

> הביאו ספרי יחוסיהם ועידי חזקת לידתם, כל אחד ואחד, להתייחס על השבט.

They brought the records of their pedigrees and witnesses of their birth claims, so that each could trace their genealogy to a tribe.

TEXT 6C

RABBI OVADIAH SEFORNO, NUMBERS 1:4

> והטעם שיהיו אתכם הוא שכל אחד מהם ראש לבית אבותיו, ולא יכחד ממנו יחס כל אחד ואחד.

The tribal princes must be at your side because each is the head of his father's home, and the pedigree of their tribesmen will be familiar to them.

Rabbi Ovadiah Seforno
1475–1550

Biblical exegete, philosopher, and physician. Seforno was born in Cesena, Italy. After gaining a thorough knowledge of Talmud and the sciences, he moved to Rome, where he studied medicine and taught Hebrew to the German scholar Johannes Reuchlin. Seforno eventually settled in Bologna, where he founded and directed a yeshiva until his death. His magnum opus is a biblical commentary focused on the simple interpretation of the text, with an emphasis on philology and philosophy.

Chain of Evidence

TEXT 6D

RABBI MOSHE SOFER, *CHATAM SOFER AL HATORAH*, NUMBERS 1:4

> ונראה לי שהיו ישראל נמנים למלך מצרים לידע כמה עבדים רומסי חומר יש, כדרך כל עבדי המלך נמנים ונכתבים בלידתם בשמם ושם אבותם.
>
> ואלו השוטרים היו משגיחים על ככה. ועל כן אמר הקדוש ברוך הוא שיקח אותן האנשים איש איש למטה במספר מפקד בני ישראל, כי אך הם יוכלו להעיד, ולהם נמסר ספר עדות לידתם בסבלות מצרים.

A suggestion: The Egyptian authorities kept records of their slaves to know the size of their available workforce. Government bureaucrats typically include names and family information in these records.

G-d instructed Moses to involve the princes in the census because they, as the Jewish foremen, managed these records in Egypt. Therefore, only they could testify to each person's pedigree, and only they had access to these Egyptian records.

Rabbi Moshe Sofer (*Chatam Sofer*)
1762–1839

A leading rabbinical authority of the 19th century. Born in Frankfurt am Main, *Chatam Sofer* ultimately accepted the rabbinate of Pressburg (now Bratislava), Slovakia. Serving as rabbi and head of the yeshiva that he established, Rabbi Sofer maintained a strong traditionalist perspective, opposing deviation from Jewish tradition. *Chatam Sofer* is the title of his collection of Halachic responsa and his commentary to the Talmud.

For the Entire Census

TEXT 7A

RASHI, NUMBERS 1:4

כשתפקדו אותם יהיו עמכם נשיא כל שבט ושבט.

When you count them, the prince of each tribe should be with you.

A Public Census

TEXT 7B

RABBI SAMSON RAPHAEL HIRSCH, NUMBERS 1:42

Out of the assembled mass of the nation, [the tribesmen of Simeon] stepped to the tribe of Simeon as belonging to him.

[This was repeated for the other tribes] so that after eleven tribes had been counted, the rest—those who had not been counted—remained by themselves as forming the twelfth tribe. And there was no necessity for them to step up to be recognized as such.

Rabbi Samson Raphael Hirsch 1808–1888

Born in Hamburg, Germany; rabbi and educator; intellectual founder of the *Torah Im Derech Eretz* school of Orthodox Judaism, which advocates combining Torah with secular education. Beginning in 1830, Hirsch served as chief rabbi in several prominent German cities. During this period, he wrote his *Nineteen Letters on Judaism*, under the pseudonym of Ben Uziel. His work helped preserve traditional Judaism during the era of the German Enlightenment. He is buried in Frankfurt am Main.

III. A NATION MEMBER, NOT A NATION-STATE

Unique but Equal

TEXT 8

THE REBBE, RABBI MENACHEM MENDEL SCHNEERSON, *LIKUTEI SICHOT* 23, P. 7

ויש לומר די הסברה פון צירוף שניהם יחד:

דאס וואס מען ציילט אידן מצד זייערע מעלות פרטיות, איז דאס ניט (נאר) בכדי ארויסצוברענגען די מעלה פון יעדן אידן (אדער שבט) פאר זיך אליין, נאר – ווי די אלע מעלות פרטיות צוזאמען שטעלן מיט זיך צונויף איין קומה שלימה.

וואס אין דעם ענין – וואס יעדע מעלה פרטית איז משלים דעם כלל – איז ניטא קיין התחלקות: פונקט ווי די "קומה שלימה" מוז אנקומען צו מעלת הראש והמוח כדי דערגרייכן איר שלימות, אזוי מוז זי אנקומען צו מעלת הרגל. און דערפאר ווערט יעדערער געציילט (גלייך) אלס איינער – ווייל אין משלים זיין דעם כלל זיינען אלע גלייך.

Rabbi Menachem Mendel Schneerson 1902–1994

The towering Jewish leader of the 20th century, known as "the Lubavitcher Rebbe," or simply as "the Rebbe." Born in southern Ukraine, the Rebbe escaped Nazi-occupied Europe, arriving in the U.S. in June 1941. The Rebbe inspired and guided the revival of traditional Judaism after the European devastation, impacting virtually every Jewish community the world over. The Rebbe often emphasized that the performance of just one additional good deed could usher in the era of Mashiach. The Rebbe's scholarly talks and writings have been printed in more than 200 volumes.

The reason both dimensions can be combined:

We count every Jew's (or tribe's) individual strengths not just to highlight their uniqueness but also because this kaleidoscope of many unique talents constitutes a single complete nation.

With respect to this point—that each unique skill completes the collective—all people, irrespective of particular skill, are equal. Just as a body requires a brain to be complete, so does it require a leg. This is why everyone is counted (equally) as one. With respect to completing the collective, all are equal.

Naming the Princes Again

TEXT 9

THE REBBE, RABBI MENACHEM MENDEL SCHNEERSON, *LIKUTEI SICHOT* 23, P. 5

על פי זה איז אויך פארשטאנדיק פארוואס דער אויבערשטער האט דא אויסגערעכנט די נעמען פון אלע נשיאים – ווייל, ווי מען האט שוין געלערנט פריער, איז דער אויבערשטער ממנה (און גיט די נויטיגע צו דעם כחות), דורך קריאה בשם, ווי עס שטייט "ראה קראתי בשם בצלאל גו' ואמלא אותו רוח אלקים גו'" (שמות לא, ב-ג).

ועל דרך זה בנידון דידן: דורך דעם וואס דער אויבערשטער האט קורא געווען די שמות הנשיאים . . . האט דאס גע'פועל'ט אין זיי א מינוי וענין חדש וואס איז בא זיי פריער ניט געווען. זיי זיינען געווארן "קרואי העדה – נקראים לכל דבר חשיבות שבעדה" (פון דער גאנצער עדה) . . .

און דערמיט ווערט אויך פארשטאנדיק דער צווייטער פסוק דא "ויקח משה ואהרן את האנשים האלה אשר נקבו בשמות" (במדבר א, יז): וויבאלד ס'איז דעמאלט נתחדש געווארן א מינוי ונתינת כוח מיוחד פון אויבערשטן צו די נשיאים, האט געדארפט אויך זיין מחדש "ויקח", אלס "קרואי העדה" (נוסף על המינוי פריער אלס נשיאי השבטים).

This explains why G-d named all the princes again. We learned earlier the notion that G-d appoints and empowers people by proclaiming their name, as it is written, "See, I have called Bezalel by name, . . . and I have imbued him with the spirit of G-d" (Exodus 31:2–3).

A similar phenomenon occurred in our case. By identifying each prince by name, G-d appointed them to a new position that they did not enjoy before. They now became leaders that the nation would call upon for every important matter.

This also explains why "Moses and Aaron took those who were indicated by name" (Numbers 1:17). Inasmuch as they were appointed to a new position—to be called upon by the nation for all important matters, in addition to their former positions as tribal princes—they needed to be drafted [by name] anew.

KEY POINTS

» Local populations must have the final say on the appointment of their leaders.

» In addition to leadership skills, leaders must be people of integrity and moral values.

» The primary duty of local leaders is to provide for the needs of their constituents.

» Nevertheless, local leaders must inculcate a sense of duty and responsibility into the entire nation.

» They do this by formulating policies that benefit not only their constituents but also the entire nation.

6.

Shavuot

Judaism: No Longer Playing Defense

Minyan *at the Airport: You In or Out?*

Dedicated to our chairman, Rabbi Moshe Kotlarsky,
as he marks his birthday, Rosh Chodesh Sivan.

May he go from strength to strength with good health, happiness,
nachas *from his loved ones, and success in all his endeavors.*
Leorech yomim veshonim tovos.

HOLIDAY OVERVIEW

Shavuot

The Torah was given by G-d to the Jewish people on Mount Sinai more than 3300 years ago. Every year, on the holiday of Shavuot, we renew our acceptance of G-d's gift, and G-d "re-gives" the Torah.

The word *shavuot* means "weeks." This holiday marks the completion of a seven-week counting period that began during Passover.

The Giving of the Torah was a far-reaching spiritual event—one that touched the essence of the Jewish soul for all times. Our sages have compared it to a wedding between G-d and the Jewish people. *Shavuot* also means "oaths," for on this day G-d swore eternal devotion to us, and we in turn pledged everlasting loyalty to Him.

In ancient times, two wheat loaves would be offered in the Holy Temple. It was also at this time that people would begin to bring *bikurim*, their first and choicest fruits, to thank G-d for Israel's bounty.

The holiday of Shavuot is a two-day holiday, beginning at sundown of the fifth day of Sivan and lasting until nightfall of the seventh day of Sivan. (In Israel it is a one-day holiday, ending at nightfall of the sixth day of Sivan.)

Women and girls light holiday candles to usher in the holiday on both the first and second evenings of the holiday.

It is customary to stay up all night learning from the Torah on the first night of Shavuot.

All men, women, and children should go to the synagogue on the first day of Shavuot to hear the reading of the Ten Commandments.

As on other holidays, special meals are eaten, and no "work" may be performed.

It is customary to eat dairy foods on Shavuot. Among other reasons, this commemorates the fact that upon receiving the Torah, including the kosher laws, the Jewish people could not cook meat in their pots, which had yet to be rendered kosher.

On the second day of Shavuot, the Yizkor memorial service is recited.

Some communities read the Book of Ruth publicly, as King David—whose passing occurred on this day—was a descendant of Ruth the Mo'abite.

INTRODUCTION

Exercise

You're in an airport and a group of Jewish men formed a minyan *with* talit, tefilin, *and the works. They aren't being obnoxious about it, nor are they overtly in anyone's way, but they aren't exactly hiding in an inconspicuous spot.*

What would you do?

1. *Join enthusiastically irrespective of what "people" might think.*
2. *Applaud silently from the side, but not join—not wanting to invite scrutiny or unwanted attention.*
3. *Feel offended or ashamed by this overt display of public "Jewishness" in a secular environment.*

In other words, would this be (a) just right, (b) a little too Jewish for you, or (c) way too Jewish for you?

I. YOUR MAJESTY

A Tale of Three Men

TEXT 1

EXODUS 19:6

וְאַתֶּם תִּהְיוּ לִי מַמְלֶכֶת כֹּהֲנִים וְגוֹי קָדוֹשׁ, אֵלֶּה הַדְּבָרִים אֲשֶׁר תְּדַבֵּר אֶל בְּנֵי יִשְׂרָאֵל.

And you shall be to Me a kingdom of princes and a holy nation.

TEXT 2

JERUSALEM TALMUD, BEITZAH 2:4

אמר רבי יוסי בי רבי בון: דוד מת בעצרת.

Rabbi Yosei the son of Boon said, "David passed away on Shavuot."

Jerusalem Talmud

A commentary to the Mishnah, compiled during the 4th and 5th centuries. The Jerusalem Talmud predates its Babylonian counterpart by 100 years and is written in both Hebrew and Aramaic. While the Babylonian Talmud is the most authoritative source for Jewish law, the Jerusalem Talmud remains an invaluable source for the spiritual, intellectual, ethical, historical, and legal traditions of Judaism.

TEXT 3

RABBI YOSEF YITZCHAK SCHNEERSOHN, *LIKUTEI DIBURIM* 2, P. 32A

אמר אחד, אשר מקובל אצל אנשי וואהלין כי הבעל שם טוב נסתלק ביום ד' לשבוע . . . ולפי זה ברור כי הסתלקות מורינו הבעל שם טוב היה ביום ראשון דחג השבועות.

There is a tradition among the Chasidim of Volhynia [a historic region in central and eastern Europe] that the Baal Shem Tov passed away on a Wednesday. . . . Accordingly, it is clear that our teacher the Baal Shem Tov passed away on the first day of Shavuot.

Rabbi Yosef Yitzchak Schneersohn (Rayatz, Frierdiker Rebbe, Previous Rebbe) 1880–1950

Chasidic rebbe, prolific writer, and Jewish activist. Rabbi Yosef Yitzchak, the sixth leader of the Chabad movement, actively promoted Jewish religious practice in Soviet Russia and was arrested for these activities. After his release from prison and exile, he settled in Warsaw, Poland, from where he fled Nazi occupation and arrived in New York in 1940. Settling in Brooklyn, Rabbi Schneersohn worked to revitalize American Jewish life. His son-in-law Rabbi Menachem Mendel Schneerson succeeded him as the leader of the Chabad movement.

TEXT 4

RABBI SHNEUR ZALMAN OF LIADI, *TANYA, IGERET HAKODESH* 28

וְהִיא עֵת רָצוֹן הַמִּתְגַּלֶּה וּמֵאִיר בִּבְחִינַת גִּילּוּי מִלְמַעְלָה לְמַטָּה, בְּעֵת פְּטִירַת צַדִּיקֵי עֶלְיוֹן עוֹבְדֵי ה' בְּאַהֲבָה, בִּמְסִירַת נַפְשָׁם לַה' בְּחַיֵּיהֶם עַרְבִית וְשַׁחֲרִית בִּקְרִיאַת שְׁמַע . . .

שֶׁכָּל עֲמַל הָאָדָם שֶׁעָמְלָה נַפְשׁוֹ בְּחַיָּיו לְמַעְלָה בִּבְחִינַת הֶעְלֵם וְהֶסְתֵּר, מִתְגַּלֶּה וּמֵאִיר בִּבְחִינַת גִּילּוּי מִלְמַעְלָה לְמַטָּה בְּעֵת פְּטִירָתוֹ.

Righteous people are those who serve G-d out of love, and who surrender their soul to G-d every morning and evening when they read the Shema. At the moment of their passing, Divine favor radiates from Above and suffuses the world below. . . .

All the sacred efforts and toil of a righteous person's lifetime [the results of which are hidden and obscured in the Heavens above] are revealed and become manifest in the world below at the time of their passing.

Rabbi Shneur Zalman of Liadi (Alter Rebbe) 1745–1812

Chasidic rebbe, Halachic authority, and founder of the Chabad movement. The Alter Rebbe was born in Liozna, Belarus, and was among the principal students of the Magid of Mezeritch. His numerous works include the *Tanya*, an early classic containing the fundamentals of Chabad Chasidism; and *Shulchan Aruch HaRav*, an expanded and reworked code of Jewish law.

A. Moses

TEXT 5

MIDRASH, *SHEMOT RABAH* 48:4

יוכבד נטלה כהונה ומלכות. אהרן - כהן גדול; משה - מלך, שנאמר: "ויהי בישורון מלך" (דברים לג, ה).

Jochebed [Moses and Aaron's mother] received priesthood and the kingdom. Aaron was appointed High Priest. Moses was appointed king, as the passage states, "He was a king in Jeshurun [Israel]" (Deuteronomy 33:5).

Shemot Rabah

An early rabbinic commentary on the Book of Exodus. "Midrash" is the designation of a particular genre of rabbinic literature usually forming a running commentary on specific books of the Bible. *Shemot Rabah*, written mostly in Hebrew, provides textual exegeses, expounds upon the biblical narrative, and develops and illustrates moral principles. It was first printed in Constantinople in 1512 together with 4 other Midrashic works on the other 4 books of the Pentateuch.

B. David

TEXT 6

MAIMONIDES, *MISHNEH TORAH*, LAWS OF KINGS AND CONQUESTS 1:7

כֵּיוָן שֶׁנִּמְשַׁח דָוִד זָכָה בְּכֶתֶר מַלְכוּת, וַהֲרֵי הַמַּלְכוּת לוֹ וּלְבָנָיו הַזְּכָרִים עַד עוֹלָם, שֶׁנֶּאֱמַר: "כִּסְאֲךָ יִהְיֶה נָכוֹן עַד עוֹלָם" . . . לֹא תִכָּרֵת הַמְּלוּכָה מִזֶּרַע דָוִד לְעוֹלָם, הַקָּדוֹשׁ בָּרוּךְ הוּא הִבְטִיחוֹ בְּכָךְ.

Once David was anointed king, he acquired the crown of kingship. Afterward, the kingship belonged to him and to his male descendants forever, as the Torah states: "Your throne will be established in perpetuity" (II Samuel 7:16).... G-d assured David that the monarchy would never be taken from his descendants.

Rabbi Moshe ben Maimon (Maimonides, Rambam) 1135–1204

Halachist, philosopher, author, and physician. Maimonides was born in Córdoba, Spain. After the conquest of Córdoba by the Almohads, he fled Spain and eventually settled in Cairo, Egypt. There, he became the leader of the Jewish community and served as court physician to the vizier of Egypt. He is most noted for authoring the *Mishneh Torah*, an encyclopedic arrangement of Jewish law; and for his philosophical work, *Guide for the Perplexed*. His rulings on Jewish law are integral to the formation of Halachic consensus.

C. The Baal Shem Tov

TEXT 7

RABBI YOSEF YITZCHAK SCHNEERSOHN, *SEFER HASICHOT* 5796, P. 195

רבינו הזקן אמר פעם: ווען דער רבי האט געוואלט מצייר זיין די רוממות פון זיידן הבעל שם טוב, אמה, כי רוממות מלך אדיר הוא כלא נגד די רוממות פון דעם רבי'ן.

The Alter Rebbe, Rabbi Shneur Zalman of Liadi, once said, "When my master [Rabbi Dov Ber of Mezeritch] wanted to describe the transcendence of my [spiritual] grandfather, the Baal Shem Tov, he would say that the exaltedness of a powerful king is nothing compared to the transcendence of the Rebbe [the Baal Shem Tov]."

Kingship Manifested

TEXT 8

THE REBBE, RABBI MENACHEM MENDEL SCHNEERSON, *LIKUTEI SICHOT* 18, PP. 37–38

וויבאלד אז משה, דוד, און דער בעל שם טוב זיינען געווען יעדערער א נשיא ומלך . . . איז פון זיי נשפע געווארען און דורכדעם ווערט נתגלה ביי יעדער אידן עניני מלך.

Moses, David, and the Baal Shem Tov were leaders and kings. With this, they endowed and revealed the capacity for kingship in every Jew.

Rabbi Menachem Mendel Schneerson 1902–1994

The towering Jewish leader of the 20th century, known as "the Lubavitcher Rebbe," or simply as "the Rebbe." Born in southern Ukraine, the Rebbe escaped Nazi-occupied Europe, arriving in the U.S. in June 1941. The Rebbe inspired and guided the revival of traditional Judaism after the European devastation, impacting virtually every Jewish community the world over. The Rebbe often emphasized that the performance of just one additional good deed could usher in the era of Mashiach. The Rebbe's scholarly talks and writings have been printed in more than 200 volumes.

II. TRANSCENDENT AND INDEPENDENT

TEXT 9

THE REBBE, RABBI MENACHEM MENDEL SCHNEERSON, *LIKUTEI SICHOT* 18, PP. 36–37

די נקודה עיקרית פון מלכות איז – התנשאות, דעם מלך'ס העכערקייט און אפגעטראגנקייט פון גאנצן פאלק; ביז אז – ער טאר זיך ניט אראפלאזן צו טאן מלאכה, מ'דארף אים צושטעלן אלע זיינע צרכים מיט גרויס הרחבה . . . קיין זאך אין דער מדינה קען ניט אפהאלטן דעם מלך פון דורכפירן זיין רצון . . .

און כעין זה האט מתן תורה אויפגעטאן ביי אידן: דורך מתן תורה איז געווארן "ורוממתנו", אידן זיינען דערהויבן געווארן . . . העכער פון וועלט . . .

אין דער עבודה פון יעדן אידן בפרט מיינט דאס: ווען עס קומט צו טאן א זאך פון תורה ומצות דארף זיך א איד פירן ווי א מלך – ער דארף זיך אפגעבן מיט דער מצוה פונקט ווי ער וואלט ניט געהאט קיינע אנדערע מלאכות ודאגות . . . קיין טבע'דיקער חשבון זאל אים ניט אפהאלטן פון צו טאן א מצוה.

The primary facet of kingship is transcendence. The monarch is exalted and above the nation, to the point that he may not lower himself to perform menial tasks. His personal needs must be provided [by the nation] without limitation. . . . No one in the country can prevent the king from doing what he wants to do.

The Jewish people were endowed with a similar capacity at Mount Sinai. The Torah raised us up high above . . . the world. . . .

This means that with respect to Torah and *mitzvot*, we must behave like kings. We must devote ourselves to *mitzvot* as if we have no other tasks or concerns on our minds. No worldly consideration should ever keep us from fulfilling a mitzvah.

Moshe Rabbeinu

TEXT 10A

TALMUD, YOMA 75A

אָמַר רַבִּי שְׁמוּאֵל בַּר נַחְמָנִי אָמַר רַבִּי יוֹנָתָן . . . שֶׁיָרְדוּ לָהֶם לְיִשְׂרָאֵל אֲבָנִים טוֹבוֹת וּמַרְגָלִיּוֹת עִם הַמָּן.

Rabbi Shmuel the son of Nachmani said in the name of Rabbi Yonasan [that] . . . precious stones and gems fell from the sky along with the manna.

Babylonian Talmud

A literary work of monumental proportions that draws upon the legal, spiritual, intellectual, ethical, and historical traditions of Judaism. The 37 tractates of the Babylonian Talmud contain the teachings of the Jewish sages from the period after the destruction of the 2nd Temple through the 5th century CE. It has served as the primary vehicle for the transmission of the Oral Law and the education of Jews over the centuries; it is the entry point for all subsequent legal, ethical, and theological Jewish scholarship.

TEXT 10B

RABBI SHALOM DOVBER SCHNEERSOHN, *KUNTRES HAAVODAH*, P. 50

דהנה דור המדבר היה להם גילוי אלקות מלמעלה בבחינת ראיה ממש מצד החיבה העליונה, וכמו שכתוב: "כבכורה בתאנה בראשיתה ראיתי אבותיכם כו'" (הושע ט, י). והיה בהם האהבה ממילא, ובבחינת דביקות ממש, בחינת אהבה בתענוגים.

The Jews in the desert could see G-d directly because He revealed Himself to them with love. They responded with spontaneous adoration in return, and cleaved to G-d with delightful love.

Rabbi Shalom Dovber Schneersohn (Rashab) 1860–1920

Chasidic rebbe. Rabbi Shalom Dovber became the 5th leader of the Chabad movement upon the passing of his father, Rabbi Shmuel Schneersohn. He established the Lubavitch network of *yeshivot* called Tomchei Temimim. He authored many volumes of Chasidic discourses and is renowned for his lucid and thorough explanations of kabbalistic concepts.

TEXT 10C

THE REBBE, RABBI MENACHEM MENDEL SCHNEERSON, *LIKUTEI SICHOT* 18, P. 42

> משה, וואס ענינו איז תורה, טוט אויף (מגלה) דעם עצם ענין פון "ממלכת כהנים"... ביי יעדן אידן אין די זמנים וואס ער גיט אפ אויף לימוד התורה - אז ער האט דעם כח זיך אויסצוטאן - באותה שעה על כל פנים - אינגאנצן פון וועלטלעכע זאכן ודאגות, און זיין אזוי צוגעטראגן צום לערנען.

Moses, whose primary element is Torah study, established and nurtured the kingship trait . . . in every Jew. When we study Torah, we can be absolutely divorced from worldly considerations and concerns and completely focus on our study.

King David

TEXT 11

THE REBBE, RABBI MENACHEM MENDEL SCHNEERSON, IBID., PP. 42–43

> דוד, וואס ענינו איז תפילה... טוט אויף... אז אויך די עבודה זאל זיין אין א מלכות'דיקן אופן: כאטש ער בעט זיינע צרכים, ווערן די בקשות נתמלא... תיכף ומיד אן קיין הגבלות ומניעות ובתכלית השלימות, ווי עס ווערט נתמלא די בקשה פון א מלך.

David's key element is prayer. He nurtured our majestic ability to pray like kings: Though we beseech G-d for our needs, our requests are instantly granted without limitation or obstacle. They are granted in full like the requests made by a king.

The Baal Shem Tov

TEXT 12A

PERETZ GOLDING, "THE BAAL SHEM TOV—A BRIEF BIOGRAPHY," WWW.CHABAD.ORG

During the late 17th century, European Jewry was still reeling from the devastation wrought by the Khmelnitsky pogroms of 5408 and 5409 (1648–1649 CE). The massacres left tens of thousands of Jews dead, and the grief-stricken survivors struggled to rebuild their broken lives and communities.

In the wake of the pogroms, the infamous Shabtai Zvi led thousands of despairing Jews to believe that he was the long-awaited Messiah destined to redeem them from exile. Many Jews were inspired with the hope that their suffering would soon end, but after Shabtai Zvi turned out to be a fraud—he converted to Islam under pressure from the Ottoman Turks—they were plunged back into the bitter reality of shtetl life.

After the pogroms, many families were left without a livelihood and the vast majority of children were forced to abandon their Torah study at a very young age, sometimes as young as five or six years old, to help provide for their families. Only the wealthy—few and far between—could afford a proper Torah education for their children. This resulted in a generation of largely ignorant, yet pious and devoted Jews who were, for the most part, neglected and scorned by the learned elite—the Talmudists. A rift developed between the learned and unlearned Jews, to the point that in many towns the two groups prayed at separate synagogues.

Against this troubling backdrop, in the small Polish town of Tloste, on the 18th of Elul, 5458 (1698), Eliezer and his wife Sarah . . . gave birth to their only child—Yisrael.

TEXT 12B

THE REBBE, RABBI MENACHEM MENDEL SCHNEERSON, *LIKUTEI SICHOT* 18, PP. 40–41

זאגט דער בעל שם טוב – אז אויך אין דער טיפעניש פון זמן הגלות קען זיך א איד אויפהויבן אינגאנצן העכער פון זיין ארום, און דערפילן ווי ער איז פון "ממלכת כהנים", וועמען דער אויבערשטער אליין *בהשגחה פרטית* בתכלית פירט באופן נסי און *בחיי יום יום* ובכל פרט ופרט . . .

ווען א איד פירט זיך מיט אזא הנהגה אין זמן הגלות, באווייזט עס ווי ער קען זיך אויפהויבן און גיין (בלשון הידוע) "לכתחילה אריבער" – ניט מיט א סדר והדרגה, נאר אינגאנצן העכער פון מדידה והגבלה – פון דער טיפעניש פון חושך הגלות צו דער הויכקייט פון "ממלכת כהנים".

The Baal Shem Tov taught that Jews can transcend their Diaspora environment even in the deepest, darkest days of Exile. We can regard ourselves as a kingdom of priests who are directed by G-d Himself with Divine providence. He guides each detail of our daily lives in a miraculous manner.

When we behave this way in Exile, we demonstrate that we can be transcendent. We can leap over all obstacles without granting them any credence—we don't climb over them step-by-step; we leap over them without measure or limitation. Thus, we transcend the depths and darkness of Exile to become a kingdom of priests.

III. WHEN G-D SETS THE STAGE

Divine Providence

TEXT 13A

RABBI YOSEF YITZCHAK SCHNEERSOHN, *LIKUTEI DIBURIM* 1, P. 83B

אלעמען איז גוט באוואוסט דער ענין פון השגחה פרטית, ווי דער בעל שם טוב איז מבאר, אז אפילו א שטרויעלע און א אפגעריסענע בלעטעלע וואס וואלגערט זיך אין גאס, איז פאראן א דין ומשפט וויפיל מאל זיי זאלן זיך אומדרעהען און וואו, אין וואסערע ערטער זיי זאלען זיך וואלגערען.

דער בעל שם טוב נשמתו עדן זאגט, אז הקדוש ברוך הוא איז מסבב כמה סיבות מסיבות שונות בכדי דורכפירן א השגחה פרטית פון א קליינעם נברא ויצור. אז בכדי אז אן אראפגעפאלענע בלעטל פון א בוים וואס וואלגערט זיך נאך פון פאראיארן ערגעץ וואו אין א הינטער הויף, אדער א שטרויעלע פון א זאנג מיט וועלכער מען האט מיט איניגע יאר פריער צוגעדעקט א דאך אין א דארף, זאלן זיך רירן פון זייערע ערטער און אריבער אין אן אנדער ארט, איז צוליב דעם ברעכט אויס אין א הייסן זונענשיינענדיגן טאג א שטורם ווינט, וואס קערט הימל און ערד, און יעמאלט ווערט דורכגעפירט די השגחה פרטית אויף דעם אראפגעפאלענע בלעטל און דער אלטער שטרויעלע.

We are all familiar with the Baal Shem Tov's teaching on Divine providence. G-d determines the precise wanderings of a little piece of hay or a leaf torn from its tree and how many times they will twist in the wind.

The Baal Shem Tov says that G-d sets many things in motion to guide the tiniest creation along its destined path. A leaf has been lying in some backyard for an entire year. A piece of hay has been serving as part of a thatched roof for several years. When they are destined to relocate, G-d breaks out a stormy wind even in the middle of a hot sunny day, overturning Heaven and earth. All this to guide a fallen leaf or old piece of hay to its providential destination.

TEXT 13B

RABBI YOSEF YITZCHAK SCHNEERSOHN, *SEFER HAMAAMARIM* 5796, P. 120

עוד זאת דתנועת הדשא הפרטי הלזה יש לו יחס כללי לכללות כונת הבריאה. דבצירוף ואיחוד כל הפעולות הפרטים של הריבוי רבבות פרטים אין מספר שישנם בכל האלפים ורבבות מינים שישנם בהד' חלוקות דדומם צומח חי מדבר, הנה נשלמה כוונה העליונה בסוד הבריאה כולה . . .

ומה אם דשא אחד פרטי, הרי גם מספר תנועותיו ואופניו הוא בא בהשגחה פרטית ונוגע להשלמת כוונת הבריאה - הנה האדם הוא ודאי שהוא מושגח בהשגחה פרטית בכל פרטי פרטיות עניני צרכיו.

Moreover, the movement of a particular blade of grass touches on the overall purpose of creation. When you combine the particular movements and functions of the endless trillions of creations of all types, the Divine purpose that undergirds all of creation is fulfilled. . . .

If the movements and direction of a single blade of grass are guided by Divine providence and impacts the overall purpose of creation, humans along with all their details and needs are certainly guided by Divine providence.

At the Airport

TEXT 14

RABBI YOSEF YITZCHAK SCHNEERSOHN, *SEFER HASICHOT* 5697, P. 191

א איד דארף וויסען אז ער גייט פון איין ארט אין דעם אנדערען, איז ניט ער גייט אליין נאר מ'פירט איהם מלמעלה.

און די כוונה איז "לשכן שמו שם" (דברים כו, א), אויף מפרסם זיין אלקות אין דעם ארט וואו ער איז.

As Jews, we must know that when we go from one place to another, we are not going on our own. We are being directed from Above.

And the intention and purpose is "to cause His Name to dwell there (Deuteronomy 26:1)"—to make G-d known in that locale.

TEXT 15

THE REBBE, RABBI MENACHEM MENDEL SCHNEERSON, *LIKUTEI SICHOT* 18, P. 40

א איד קען מיינען, אז אין אזא צייט, ווען ס'זיינען דא אזויפיל העלמות והסתרים אויף קיום התורה ומצוות, איז די והותר אויב ער וועט מקיים זיין תורה ומצוות על דרך הרגיל (וואס אויך דאס איז פארבונדן מיט א שווערער מלחמה און מיט פיל יגיעה צו בייקומען די שוועריקייטן וכו׳) . . .

ווי קען מען אבער אין אזא זמן זיך אפגעבן מיט תורה ומצוות ווי איינער פון "ממלכת כהנים" – כאילו ווי דער גאנצער העלם ובלבול איז ניטא במציאות?!

A Jew might think, at a time when there are so many challenges against observing Torah and *mitzvot*, it is enough to practice in a normal way (which is hard enough and often entails extreme effort).

How can we commit ourselves to practicing the Torah and *mitzvot* like a kingdom of priests under such circumstances? How can we act as if the entire world and its hubbub don't exist?

Conclusion: Lights, Camera, Action

TEXT 16

RABBI YOSEF YITZCHAK SCHNEERSOHN, *IGROT KODESH* 6, PP. 407–408

המאמין בהשגחה פרטית יודע כי "מה' מצעדי גבר כוננו" (תהלים לז, כג), אשר נשמה זו צריכה לברר ולתקן איזה בירור ותיקון במקום פלוני.

ומאות בשנים, או גם משעת בריאת העולם, הנה הדבר שצריך להתברר או להתתקן מחכה לאותה הנשמה שתבוא לבררו ולתקנו. וגם נשמה הלזו, הנה מאז נאצלה ונבראה היא מחכה לזמן ירידתה, לברר ולתקן את אשר הוטל עליה . . .

בלי שום צל ספק וספק ספיקא, הנה בכל מקום מדרך כף רגלינו . . . הכל הוא לזכות ולטהר את הארץ באותיות התורה והתפלה. ואנחנו כל ישראל הנה שלוחי דרחמנא אנחנו, איש איש כאשר גזרה עליו ההשגחה העליונה.

אין חפשי מעבודת הקודש אשר הועמסה על שכמנו.

Whoever believes in individual Divine providence knows that "man's steps are established by G-d" (Psalms 37:23), that this particular soul must purify and improve something specific in a particular place.

For centuries, or even since the world's Creation, that which needs purification or improvement has waited for this soul to come and purify or improve it. The soul, too, has waited since it came into being for its time to descend to this world and discharge the purification and improvement missions assigned to it. . . .

There is not the vaguest shadow of doubt that wherever our feet tread, . . . it is all to cleanse and purify the world with words of Torah and prayer. We, all of Israel, are emissaries of G-d, each as Divine providence has decreed for us.

No one is free from this sacred task that was placed on our shoulders.

KEY POINTS

» On Shavuot, G-d declared all Jews a kingdom of priests. This means that we each have the kingship trait within us.

» The kingship trait translates into an ability to do G-d's bidding at all times and places without concern about what others might think or say. Nothing gets in a king's way.

» We are aided and supported in this by three great Jewish kings who are all linked to Shavuot: Moses, King David, and Rabbi Yisrael Baal Shem Tov, founder of Chasidism.

» Moses taught us to divorce ourselves from the world while we study Torah. David taught us how to pray with absolute confidence.

» The Baal Shem Tov exemplified the idea that our kingship prevails even in the darkest of times.

» The Baal Shem Tov further taught that every encounter is orchestrated by G-d to help us serve Him. And so, we should lead our lives with the attitude that the world is on our side.

7. Naso

Unleash Your Power

Every Individual Is an Entire Collective

Dedicated in loving memory of Sr. Mijal Stabinski,
מיכאל בן שבתי,
marking his yahrtzeit *on 9 Sivan.*

May the merit of the Torah study worldwide accompany his soul in the world of everlasting life and be a source of blessings to his family, with much health, happiness, nachas, *and success.*

PARSHAH OVERVIEW

Naso

Completing the head count of the Children of Israel taken in the Sinai Desert, a total of 8,580 Levite men between the ages of thirty and fifty are counted in a tally of those who will be doing the actual work of transporting the Tabernacle.

G-d communicates to Moses the law of the *sotah*, the wayward wife suspected of unfaithfulness to her husband. Also given is the law of the *nazir*, who forswears wine, lets his or her hair grow long, and is forbidden to become contaminated through contact with a dead body. Aaron and his descendants, the *Kohanim*, are instructed on how to bless the people of Israel.

The leaders of the twelve tribes of Israel each bring their offerings for the inauguration of the altar. Although their gifts are identical, each is brought on a different day and is individually described by the Torah.

INTRODUCTION

Question for Discussion

What factors could prevent us from following through with a life change we seriously intend to implement?

I. EFRAIM'S AMBIGUOUS OFFERING

The Princes and Their Offerings

TEXT 1A

NUMBERS 7:1–3

א. וַיְהִי בְּיוֹם כַּלּוֹת מֹשֶׁה לְהָקִים אֶת הַמִּשְׁכָּן, וַיִּמְשַׁח אֹתוֹ וַיְקַדֵּשׁ אֹתוֹ וְאֶת כָּל כֵּלָיו וְאֶת הַמִּזְבֵּחַ וְאֶת כָּל כֵּלָיו, וַיִּמְשָׁחֵם וַיְקַדֵּשׁ אֹתָם.

ב. וַיַּקְרִיבוּ נְשִׂיאֵי יִשְׂרָאֵל רָאשֵׁי בֵּית אֲבֹתָם, הֵם נְשִׂיאֵי הַמַּטֹּת, הֵם הָעֹמְדִים עַל הַפְּקֻדִים.

ג. וַיָּבִיאוּ אֶת קָרְבָּנָם לִפְנֵי ה', שֵׁשׁ עֶגְלֹת צָב וּשְׁנֵי עָשָׂר בָּקָר, עֲגָלָה עַל שְׁנֵי הַנְּשִׂאִים וְשׁוֹר לְאֶחָד, וַיַּקְרִיבוּ אוֹתָם לִפְנֵי הַמִּשְׁכָּן.

1. And it was that on the day that Moses finished setting up the Mishkan, he anointed it, sanctified it, along with all its vessels, and the altar with all its vessels; and he anointed them and sanctified them.

2. The princes of Israel, the heads of their fathers' houses, presented [their offerings]. They were the leaders of the tribes. They were the ones who would be present during the head count.

3. They brought their offering before G-d: six covered wagons and twelve oxen, a wagon for every two chieftains, and an ox for each one; they presented them in front of the Mishkan.

TEXT 1B

IBID., 7:48

> בַּיּוֹם הַשְּׁבִיעִי נָשִׂיא לִבְנֵי אֶפְרָיִם, אֱלִישָׁמָע בֶּן עַמִּיהוּד.

On the seventh day, the prince of Efraim, Elishama ben Amihud, [brought his offering].

A Private Offering on Shabbat?

TEXT 2

TALMUD, TEMURAH 14A

> יש בקרבנות הציבור מה שאין בקרבנות יחיד, שקרבנות הציבור דוחין את השבת ואת הטומאה, וקרבנות יחיד אינן דוחות לא את השבת ולא את הטומאה.

There are *Halachot* that apply to communal offerings that do not apply to private offerings: communal offerings override Shabbat and ritual impurity [i.e., they are sacrificed even if the priests are impure], and private offerings override neither Shabbat nor ritual impurity.

Babylonian Talmud

A literary work of monumental proportions that draws upon the legal, spiritual, intellectual, ethical, and historical traditions of Judaism. The 37 tractates of the Babylonian Talmud contain the teachings of the Jewish sages from the period after the destruction of the 2nd Temple through the 5th century CE. It has served as the primary vehicle for the transmission of the Oral Law and the education of Jews over the centuries; it is the entry point for all subsequent legal, ethical, and theological Jewish scholarship.

TEXT 3

RASHI, NUMBERS 7:14

"מלאה קטורת". לא מצינו קטורת ליחיד ולא על מזבח החיצון - אלא זו בלבד, והוראת שעה היתה.

"A gold spoon filled with incense . . ." We never find a private offering of incense, nor incense burned atop the outer altar, except for this once. This exception was temporarily authorized.

Rabbi Shlomo Yitzchaki (Rashi)
1040–1105

Most noted biblical and Talmudic commentator. Born in Troyes, France, Rashi studied in the famed *yeshivot* of Mainz and Worms. His commentaries on the Pentateuch and the Talmud, which focus on the straightforward meaning of the text, appear in virtually every edition of the Talmud and Bible.

A Strange Reward

TEXT 4

MIDRASH, *BAMIDBAR RABAH* 14:2

"מִי הִקְדִימַנִי וַאֲשַׁלֵּם" (אִיּוֹב מא, ג)? מְדַבֵּר בְּיוֹסֵף, שֶׁהוּא הִקְדִים וְשָׁמַר אֶת הַשַּׁבָּת עַד שֶׁלֹּא נִתְּנָה. "וּטְבֹחַ טֶבַח וְהָכֵן" (בְּרֵאשִׁית מג, טז), אָמַר רַבִּי יוֹחָנָן: עֶרֶב שַׁבָּת הָיְתָה, וְאֵין הָכֵן אֶלָּא לְשַׁבָּת, שֶׁנֶּאֱמַר: "וְהָיָה בַּיּוֹם הַשִּׁשִּׁי וְהֵכִינוּ וְגוֹ'" (שְׁמוֹת טז, ה).

אָמַר הַקָּדוֹשׁ בָּרוּךְ הוּא: יוֹסֵף, אַתָּה שָׁמַרְתָּ אֶת הַשַּׁבָּת עַד שֶׁלֹּא נִתְּנָה הַתּוֹרָה, חַיֶּיךָ שֶׁאֲנִי מְשַׁלֵּם לְבֶן בִּנְךָ שֶׁיְּהֵא מַקְרִיב קָרְבָּנוֹ בַּשַּׁבָּת מַה שֶּׁאֵין יָחִיד מַקְרִיב, וְעָלַי לְקַבֵּל קָרְבָּנוֹ בְּרָצוֹן!

הֱוֵי: "מִי הִקְדִימַנִי וַאֲשַׁלֵּם". וּמִנַּיִן שֶׁכֵּן הוּא? מִמַּה שֶּׁאָמוּר בָּעִנְיָן: "בַּיּוֹם הַשְּׁבִיעִי נָשִׂיא לִבְנֵי אֶפְרָיִם וְגוֹ'".

"Who acted before me? I will repay him" (Job 41:3). This is a reference to Joseph, who acted ahead of his time and kept Shabbat before G-d commanded it. When his brothers came to Egypt, [Joseph] commanded his servants, "Slaughter an animal and prepare it" (Genesis 43:16). Rabbi Yochanan said, "It was Friday, and Joseph prepared it for Shabbat, as the word 'prepare' connotes Shabbat, as in, 'On the sixth day, they will prepare' (Exodus 16:5)."

G-d said, "Joseph, you kept Shabbat before the Torah commanded it, so I swear I will repay your grandson: he will bring his offering on Shabbat when no private offering is brought, and I will accept his offering with favor."

This is a case of "Who acted before me? I will repay him." And where did G-d keep his promise? Thus it says, "On the seventh day, the prince of Efraim . . ."

Bamidbar Rabah

An exegetical commentary on the 1st 7 chapters of the Book of Numbers and a homiletic commentary on the rest of the book. The first part of *Bamidbar Rabah* is notable for its inclusion of esoteric material; the second half is essentially identical to *Midrash Tanchuma* on the book of Numbers. It was first printed in Constantinople in 1512, together with 4 other midrashic works on the other four books of the Pentateuch.

TEXT 5

THE REBBE, RABBI MENACHEM MENDEL SCHNEERSON, *LIKUTEI SICHOT* 23, P. 47

> איז תמוה: ווי פאסט צו זאגן, אז דער שכר אויף שמירת שבת איז - "שיהא מקריב קרבנו בשבת מה שאין יחיד מקריב כו'" - א פעולה וועלכע איז (בכלל) דער היפך פון שמירת שבת?!

It is strange: How does it make sense that the reward for keeping Shabbat is, "He will bring his offering on Shabbat, when no private offering is brought," an action that is in direct opposition to observing Shabbat?

Rabbi Menachem Mendel Schneerson 1902–1994

The towering Jewish leader of the 20th century, known as "the Lubavitcher Rebbe," or simply as "the Rebbe." Born in southern Ukraine, the Rebbe escaped Nazi-occupied Europe, arriving in the U.S. in June 1941. The Rebbe inspired and guided the revival of traditional Judaism after the European devastation, impacting virtually every Jewish community the world over. The Rebbe often emphasized that the performance of just one additional good deed could usher in the era of Mashiach. The Rebbe's scholarly talks and writings have been printed in more than 200 volumes.

II. LEADERS TRANSFORMING CHALLENGES

Private Individual or Leader?

TEXT 6

RASHI, NUMBERS 21:21

הנשיא הוא הכל.

The *nasi* is the whole community.

TEXT 7

THE REBBE, RABBI MENACHEM MENDEL SCHNEERSON, *SICHOT KODESH* 5741:3, P. 66

דער קרבן הנשיא בכל יום איז געווען א קרבן יחיד, און אף על פי כן איז דאס געווען פארבונדן מיט, און אין דעם איז געווען תלוי - א רבים, און ביז ווי מ'זאגט "הנשיא הוא הכל".

The offerings the princes brought each day were private offerings. Nevertheless, these offerings were inherently bound to a public that participated in them by extension, so much so that we can say "the *nasi* is the whole community."

Who Was Efraim?

TEXT 8

GENESIS 41:50, 52

נ. וּלְיוֹסֵף יֻלַּד שְׁנֵי בָנִים . . .

נב. וְאֵת שֵׁם הַשֵּׁנִי קָרָא אֶפְרָיִם, כִּי הִפְרַנִי אֱלֹקִים בְּאֶרֶץ עָנְיִי.

50. Two sons were born to Joseph. . . .

52. And the second one he named Efraim, [saying,] "G-d made me fruitful in the land of my impoverishment."

Efraim, Joseph, and Spiritual Adversity

TEXT 9

THE REBBE, RABBI MENACHEM MENDEL SCHNEERSON, *LIKUTEI SICHOT* 15, P. 433

ער איז (און זיין עבודה איז) אין "ארץ עניי", אין דעם חושך הגלות - ביז אין אן אופן, אז ביי אים איז ניטא (אויף אזויפיל) דער זכרון פון "בית אבי" - און דארטן הארעוועט ער (צו באלייכטן דעם חושך הגלות מיטן אור הקדושה; און דורכדעם ווערט אויפגעטאן אן עילוי ויתרון אויך אין דעם אדם העובד) ביז אז - "הפרני אלקים (דוקא) בארץ עניי".

Efraim's life's mission is in "a land of impoverishment," in the darkness of Exile. He is in a darkness so intense, he no longer (readily) remembers his "father's home." But there he works to enlighten the darkness of Exile with spiritual light. This work brings him spiritual growth and advantage—to the point where he can say, "G-d made me fruitful (specifically) in the land of my impoverishment."

TEXT 10

THE REBBE, RABBI MENACHEM MENDEL SCHNEERSON, *SICHOT KODESH* 5741:3, P. 68

היינטיקע צייטן דארף מען ניט זוכן וואו עס איז דער ענין פון "עניי", ווארום מ'איז דאך אין גלות, וואס גלות איז דאך ענין העוני, און אין גלות גופא איז כמאמר רבותינו ז"ל: "אין עני אלא בדיעה", פעלט איצטער דער "דע את אלקי אביך ועבדהו בלבב שלם" וואס דאס איז דער דעת פון א אידן.

און אף על פי כן זאגט מען, אז אין דעם "ארץ עניי" איז דא דער "הפרני", אז ניט נאר עס ווערט ניט קיין חסרון דורך דעם וואס מ'געפינט זיך "בארץ עניי", נאר אדרבה - עס ווערט "הפרני", אז דוקא דורך דעם וואס מ'געפינט זיך "בארץ עניי", ווערט כלשון הידוע "יתרון האור מן החושך".

דאס הייסט בפשטות, אז ער ווערט ניט נתפעל דערפון וואס ער געפינט זיך "בארץ עניי", ער געפינט זיך אין מצרים, ועל דרך זה אין דעם איצטיקן גלות, ואדרבה דורך דעם איז ער מוסיף בעבודתו, עס ווערט דער "הפרני".

Nowadays, we don't need to seek out "poverty"; after all, we find ourselves in Exile, and Exile is defined by "impoverishment." More specifically, as our sages say, "Poverty is a state of mind" [Talmud, Nedarim 41a]. Indeed, today we lack the aptitude to "know the G-d of [our] father and serve Him with a full heart" [I Chronicles 28:9', which is the Jewish people's natural wisdom.

Nevertheless, we are resolute in our knowledge that this "impoverished land" is really a source of "fruitfulness." Not only do our poor circumstances not detract from our ability to flourish spiritually, to the contrary, they generate "fruitfulness." Specifically because we find ourselves in an "impoverished land," we can create "a greater light that emerges from darkness" [Ecclesiastes 2:13].

Simply speaking this means: when we refuse to be moved by the "impoverished land" we find ourselves in, be it the "land of Egypt" or our own Exile, standing up to the challenge it presents contributes to our growth and yields spiritual "fruit."

III. EMBRACING OUR INFLUENCE

Beyond Personal Growth

TEXT 11

THE REBBE, RABBI MENACHEM MENDEL SCHNEERSON, *SICHOT KODESH* 5741:3, P. 67

בשעת ער גיט א טראכט אז יעדער פעולה וואס ער טוט איז נוגע צו "הכל" - איז פועל אז ער זאל זיך ניט אפזאגן זיך פון טאן א פעולה טובה צוליב שווערקייטן, אדער זיך בכלל רעכענען מיט שווערקייטן, ווארום במה נחשב די שווערקייט וואס ער האט לגבי דעם וואס ער טוט אויף דורך די פעולה פאר "הכל", פאר כל העולם כולו, ביז אויך פאר "שכינתא בגלותא".

When we realize that every action we undertake impacts "the whole," it makes us realize that we cannot afford to defer positive action on account of the difficulties it presents. We cease even to account for the difficulties. Of what significance are these challenges when compared to the impact our action will have on "the whole," the entire world, and even G-d Himself?

TEXT 12

THE REBBE, RABBI MENACHEM MENDEL SCHNEERSON, IBID., PP. 66–67

אף על פי אז ער ווייס זיין מעמד ומצב, אז ס'איז לכאורה ווייט פון דעם ענין פון "הנשיא הוא הכל" - אף על פי כן, האט ער אין זיך א חלק אלוקה ממעל ממש, וכלשון הידוע "כשאתה תופס במקצת מן העצם אתה תופס בכולו", אז ער האט א מקצת פון דעם עצם - האט ער דער גאנצער עצם, איז וויבאלד אז ער האט אין זיך א חלק אלוקה - איז דאס ווי ער וואלט געהאט "כולו" כביכול, איז ער במילא שייך צו דעם ענין פון "הנשיא הוא הכל".

We all know the truth about ourselves; we're far from the ideal of a "leader who contains the whole." Nonetheless, we contain a "literal piece of G-d above." So, inasmuch as the Baal Shem Tov taught, "When you grasp a piece of G-d's essence, you grasp all of Him," we have access to the entire "essence." Inherently, this then means that the ideal typified by "the leader is the whole" is relevant to us.

TEXT 13

THE REBBE, RABBI MENACHEM MENDEL SCHNEERSON,
TORAT MENACHEM 5741:3, P. 70

וואס כל זה איז די הוראה פון הקרבת הקרבן פון דעם נשיא לבני אפרים, אז אף על פי אז ער איז "בארץ עניי" קומט ער צו נאך העכער ווי (די השראת השכינה אין) דעם בית המקדש.

This is the lesson we can take from the offering brought by the leader of the tribe of Efraim: even when we find ourselves in a spiritually "impoverished land," we can rise yet higher, to the place where the Divine Presence rests, the Holy Temple.

Offering the Finest Reward

TEXT 14

THE REBBE, RABBI MENACHEM MENDEL SCHNEERSON, *LIKUTEI SICHOT* 23, P. 52

> און דעריבער, איז דוקא ביי אים געווען דער ענין פון הקרבת הקרבן בשבת, אז פון אן עניין של הקרבה, וואס ביום השבת איז דאס לכאורה אן ענין פון "עניי" - ווערט פארקערט, "הפרני", א תוספת אין (שמירת ו)קדושת שבת.

[Efraim's prince] in particular was chosen to bring his offering on Shabbat because it represented his ability to transform the act of bringing an offering, which on the face of it is "an impoverishment" of Shabbat, into a "fruitful" act that adds to the observance and sanctity of Shabbat.

Recognizing Our Impact

TEXT 15A

RABBI YOSEF YITZCHAK SCHNEERSOHN, *SEFER HAMAAMARIM* 5710, P. 190

> יעדער יחיד איז א רבים, ער איז בכח צו מאכן א רבים און באלעבן א רבים.

Every individual is a community; they have the power to create a community and to bring life to a community.

Rabbi Yosef Yitzchak Schneersohn (Rayatz, Frierdiker Rebbe, Previous Rebbe) 1880–1950

Chasidic rebbe, prolific writer, and Jewish activist. Rabbi Yosef Yitzchak, the 6th leader of the Chabad movement, actively promoted Jewish religious practice in Soviet Russia and was arrested for these activities. After his release from prison and exile, he settled in Warsaw, Poland, from where he fled Nazi occupation and arrived in New York in 1940. Settling in Brooklyn, Rabbi Schneersohn worked to revitalize American Jewish life. His son-in-law Rabbi Menachem Mendel Schneerson succeeded him as the leader of the Chabad movement.

TEXT 15B

THE REBBE, RABBI MENACHEM MENDEL SCHNEERSON, *IGROT KODESH* 3, P. 267

הורו לנו נשיאינו בכלל ונשיא דורנו, הוא כבוד קדושת מורי וחמי אדוננו מורנו ורבינו . . . בפרט, אשר צריך להשתדל בטובה - גשמיית ורוחניית - גם של יחיד בכל תוקף ועוז. ומובנה הוראה זו, כי הרי אין אתנו יודע איזה יכשר ואם כלם כאחד טובים. ומלבד זה שנפש אחת מישראל עולם מלא היא מצד עצמה, הנה נתבאר בשיחה הנדפסת בקונטרס [שיחת אחרון של פסח תש"ט] . . . אשר יעדער יחיד איז א רבים, ער איז בכח צו מאכן א רבים און באלעבן א רבים.

זאת אומרת, אשר גם אם נמצא בין המושפעים שלו איש אשר בטבעו מתבודד הוא, א פארזיך'דיגער, הרי אין זה אלא מצד טבעו קודם העבודה בעצמו, ומי יודע באיזה מעמד ומצב יהיה מחר ולאחר זמן.

Our teachers, and especially the leader in our generation, my father-in-law the [Previous] Rebbe, taught that we must begin by working for the physical and spiritual welfare of the individuals around us with all our energy. This teaching is understandable, for we don't know which of our efforts will succeed, or if they will all come to good. We only know that every Jewish soul is a full world unto itself, as the Previous Rebbe said, "Every individual is a community; they have the power to create a community and to bring life to a community."

This means that even if there is a person you influence who does not engage with the community, and is "out for themselves," that's only how their nature is before they begin to work on themselves, and who knows what [leadership qualities] may come of such people after a time?

KEY POINTS

- » The offering brought by the leader of Efraim on the first Shabbat after the Mishkan's inauguration seems to violate the laws of Shabbat.
- » The Midrash says he was allowed to bring this offering on Shabbat as a reward to Yosef, who kept Shabbat while in Egypt. But this seems counterintuitive.
- » Rashi explains that Jewish leaders are considered equivalent to the whole of the community they serve. This makes the offerings the leaders brought closer to "communal offerings," and apparently permitted on Shabbat.
- » The name Efraim reflects Joseph's ability to be spiritually "fruitful" even while grappling with spiritual adversity in "the land of impoverishment."
- » Joseph and Efraim's approach to spiritual growth rejects the idea that we need to avoid sources of challenge. Instead, it transforms spiritual challenges into allies.
- » They overcame challenges by embracing the power they had to transform their circumstances and assume a leadership role.
- » The leader of Efraim's offering demonstrated the ability to transform the apparently negative into positivity, making his reward the ideal one for the approach that led Joseph to keep Shabbat in Egypt.
- » We can overcome feelings of inadequacy by recognizing our power to influence others and embracing a leadership role.
- » By seeking the physical and spiritual welfare of those around us, we can realize our latent potential to "create a community and give life to a community."

8.

Behaalotecha

Passing Up the Bonus

If It Costs the People, It's Not Worth the Gain

Dedicated in loving memory of Asya Bas Bentzion,
אסיא בת בנציון,
marking her yahrtzeit *on 18 Sivan.*

May the merit of the Torah study worldwide accompany her soul in the world of everlasting life and be a source of blessings to her family, with much health, happiness, nachas, *and success.*

PARSHAH OVERVIEW

Behaalotecha

Aaron is commanded to raise light in the lamps of the *menorah*, and the tribe of Levi is initiated into the service in the Sanctuary.

A "second Passover" is instituted in response to the petition, "Why should we be deprived?" by a group of Jews who were unable to bring the Passover offering in its appointed time because they were ritually impure. G-d instructs Moses on the procedures for Israel's journeys and encampments in the desert, and the people journey in formation from Mount Sinai, where they had been camped for nearly a year. The people are dissatisfied with their "bread from Heaven" (the manna), and demand that Moses supply them with meat. Moses appoints seventy elders, to whom he imparts of his spirit, to assist him in the burden of governing the people. Miriam speaks negatively of Moses and is punished with leprosy; Moses prays for her healing, and the entire community waits seven days for her recovery.

INTRODUCTION

Question for Discussion

Suppose your community has the opportunity to move to Israel and reestablish the community there. However, not enough members of the community want to move. Should the rabbi move and hope that the others will follow, or should the rabbi stay behind with the community? Should leaders rise to the occasion or remain with their people?

I. THE FIRST PASSOVER

A Unique Commandment

TEXT 1A

NUMBERS 9:1–2

> א. וַיְדַבֵּר ה' אֶל מֹשֶׁה בְמִדְבַּר סִינַי בַּשָּׁנָה הַשֵּׁנִית לְצֵאתָם מֵאֶרֶץ מִצְרַיִם, בַּחֹדֶשׁ הָרִאשׁוֹן לֵאמֹר:
>
> ב. וְיַעֲשׂוּ בְנֵי יִשְׂרָאֵל אֶת הַפָּסַח בְּמוֹעֲדוֹ:

1. G-d spoke to Moses in the Sinai desert in the first month of the second year of their Exodus from Egypt, saying:

2. "The Children of Israel should bring the paschal offering in its appointed time."

TEXT 1B

NUMBERS 9:5

> וַיַּעֲשׂוּ אֶת הַפֶּסַח בָּרִאשׁוֹן בְּאַרְבָּעָה עָשָׂר יוֹם לַחֹדֶשׁ בֵּין הָעַרְבַּיִם בְּמִדְבַּר סִינָי, כְּכֹל אֲשֶׁר צִוָּה ה' אֶת מֹשֶׁה כֵּן עָשׂוּ בְּנֵי יִשְׂרָאֵל:

And the Children of Israel brought the paschal offering in the Sinai desert in the afternoon of the fourteenth day of the month. They did it in accordance with all that G-d had instructed Moses.

TEXT 1C

SIFREI, AD LOC.

להודיע שבחן של ישראל, שכשם שאמר להם משה כן עשו.

This was said in praise of the Israelites. They did precisely as Moses had instructed.

Sifrei

An early rabbinic Midrash on the biblical books of Numbers and Deuteronomy. *Sifrei* focuses mostly on matters of law, as opposed to narratives and moral principles. According to Maimonides, this Halachic Midrash was authored by Rav, a 3rd-century Babylonian Talmudic sage.

A Showcase of Love

TEXT 2

NUMBERS 9:6–7

ו. וַיְהִי אֲנָשִׁים אֲשֶׁר הָיוּ טְמֵאִים לְנֶפֶשׁ אָדָם וְלֹא יָכְלוּ לַעֲשֹׂת הַפֶּסַח בַּיּוֹם הַהוּא, וַיִּקְרְבוּ לִפְנֵי מֹשֶׁה וְלִפְנֵי אַהֲרֹן בַּיּוֹם הַהוּא:

ז. וַיֹּאמְרוּ הָאֲנָשִׁים הָהֵמָּה אֵלָיו אֲנַחְנוּ טְמֵאִים לְנֶפֶשׁ אָדָם, לָמָּה נִגָּרַע לְבִלְתִּי הַקְרִיב אֶת קָרְבַּן ה' בְּמֹעֲדוֹ בְּתוֹךְ בְּנֵי יִשְׂרָאֵל:

6. Several men were in a state of ritual contamination by virtue of contact with a dead body and were thus unable to bring the paschal offering on that day. They approached Moses and Aaron on that day.

7. And they said to them, “We are impure by virtue of contact with a dead body; why should we lose out and be unable to bring the offering to G-d among the Children of Israel at the appointed time?”

The Chronology

TEXT 3

NUMBERS 1:1–2

> א. וַיְדַבֵּר ה' אֶל מֹשֶׁה בְּמִדְבַּר סִינַי בְּאֹהֶל מוֹעֵד, בְּאֶחָד לַחֹדֶשׁ הַשֵּׁנִי בַּשָּׁנָה הַשֵּׁנִית לְצֵאתָם מֵאֶרֶץ מִצְרַיִם לֵאמֹר:
>
> ב. שְׂאוּ אֶת רֹאשׁ כָּל עֲדַת בְּנֵי יִשְׂרָאֵל לְמִשְׁפְּחֹתָם לְבֵית אֲבֹתָם, בְּמִסְפַּר שֵׁמוֹת כָּל זָכָר לְגֻלְגְּלֹתָם:

1. On the first day of the second month of the second year after the Exodus from Egypt, G-d spoke to Moses in the Sinai desert, in the Tent of Meeting, saying:

2. "Count the congregation of the Children of Israel by families following their fathers' houses, a head count of every male according to the number of their names."

TEXT 4A

RASHI, NUMBERS 9:1

> אין סדר מוקדם ומאוחר בתורה.

The order of events in the Torah is not chronological.

Rabbi Shlomo Yitzchaki (Rashi)
1040–1105

Most noted biblical and Talmudic commentator. Born in Troyes, France, Rashi studied in the famed *yeshivot* of Mainz and Worms. His commentaries on the Pentateuch and the Talmud, which focus on the straightforward meaning of the text, appear in virtually every edition of the Talmud and Bible.

TEXT 4B

NACHMANIDES, BAMIDBAR 16:1

כל התורה כסדר, זולתי במקום אשר יפרש הכתוב ההקדמה והאחור,
וגם שם - לצורך ענין ולטעם נכון.

The entire Torah is in chronological order except for those occasions when the Torah specifies that the dates are out of order. Even in those cases, it is for good reason and proper purpose.

Rabbi Moshe ben Nachman (Nachmanides, Ramban) 1194–1270

Scholar, philosopher, author, and physician. Nachmanides was born in Spain and served as leader of Iberian Jewry. In 1263, he was summoned by King James of Aragon to a public disputation with Pablo Cristiani, a Jewish apostate. Though Nachmanides was the clear victor of the debate, he had to flee Spain because of the resulting persecution. He moved to Israel and helped reestablish communal life in Jerusalem. He authored a classic commentary on the Pentateuch and a commentary on the Talmud.

II. A SHAMEFUL EPISODE

Open with Love

TEXT 5

RASHI, GENESIS 1:1

> אם יאמרו אומות העולם לישראל: "לסטים אתם" שכבשתם ארצות שבעה גוים", הם אומרים להם: "כל הארץ של הקדוש ברוך הוא היא. הוא בראה ונתנה לאשר ישר בעיניו - ברצונו נתנה להם, וברצונו נטלה מהם ונתנה לנו".

Should the nations ever accuse the Jews of stealing Israel, the land of the seven nations, the Jews will respond, "The whole world belongs to G-d. He created it and gave it to the people He chose. It was His choice to gift it to them, and it was also His choice to take it from them and gift it to us."

TEXT 6

RASHI, NUMBERS 1:1

מתוך חיבתן לפניו מונה אותם כל שעה.

כשיצאו ממצרים מנאן, וכשנפלו בעגל מנאן לידע מנין הנותרים. כשבא להשרות שכינתו עליהן מנאן. באחד בניסן הוקם המשכן, ובאחד באייר מנאם.

G-d counts the Jews all the time because He loves them.

When they emerged from [bondage in] Egypt, G-d counted them. After they worshipped the Golden Calf and many died in a plague, G-d counted them to determine how many had survived. The Tabernacle was erected on the first of Nisan, and indeed, on the first of the [following month] Iyar, G-d counted them.

A Better Love Story

TEXT 7

THE REBBE, RABBI MENACHEM MENDEL SCHNEERSON,
LIKUTEI SICHOT 23, PP. 68–69

דער מעלה וחיבה פון אידן אין דעם וואס דער אויבערשטער האט זיי דאן אנגעזאגט (אחרי הקמת המשכן) א מצוה מיוחדת, וואס מצד עצמה זיינען זיי דעמולט (אין מדבר) ניט געווען מחוייב, וואס דאס אליין ווייזט שוין אויף שבחן וחיבתן של ישראל.

און די אידן האבן מקיים געווען די מצוה, און מקריב געווען דעם קרבן אין משכן בשלימות "ככל אשר צוה ה' את משה כן עשו בני ישראל", כנזכר לעיל.

נאך מערעה, דא דריקט זיך אויס די מעלה ושבח פון אידן – ווי שטארק זיי האבן געוואלט מקיים זיין ציווי ה', אז אפילו "אנשים אשר היו טמאים לנפש אדם ולא יכלו לעשות הפסח", אויך זיי האבן געמאנט און גע'טענה'ט "למה נגרע לבלתי הקריב את קרבן ה' במועדו".

און די חיבה פון אידן ביים אויבערשטן, אז ער האט אנגענומען זייער טענה ובקשה "למה נגרע" און געגעבן זיי די געלעגנהייט צו משלים זיין דעם חסרון און מקריב זיין דעם קרבן פסח שני.

G-d issued a special commandment (after the Tabernacle was erected) from which the Jews were otherwise exempt (in the desert). This demonstrates their greatness and G-d's love for them.

[Then there is the fact] that Jews fulfilled this commandment perfectly, "in accordance with all that G-d had commanded Moses."

Moreover, this story flatters the Jews by demonstrating just how much they yearned to fulfill this commandment. Even "those who were impure by virtue of contact with a dead body and could not bring the offering" demanded and argued,

Rabbi Menachem Mendel Schneerson 1902–1994

The towering Jewish leader of the 20th century, known as "the Lubavitcher Rebbe," or simply as "the Rebbe." Born in southern Ukraine, the Rebbe escaped Nazi-occupied Europe, arriving in the U.S. in June 1941. The Rebbe inspired and guided the revival of traditional Judaism after the European devastation, impacting virtually every Jewish community the world over. The Rebbe often emphasized that the performance of just one additional good deed could usher in the era of Mashiach. The Rebbe's scholarly talks and writings have been printed in more than 200 volumes.

"Why should we lose out from bringing this offering in its appointed time?"

G-d's love for the Jews is further expressed by the fact that G-d accepted the demand and entreaty, "Why should we lose out?" He granted them the opportunity to fill in the gap by providing a makeup date for the paschal offering.

Potential Risk

TEXT 8

RASHI, NUMBERS 9:1

ולמה לא פתח בזו?

מפני שהוא גנותן של ישראל, שכל ארבעים שנה שהיו ישראל במדבר לא הקריבו אלא פסח זה בלבד.

Why did the Torah not begin with the paschal offering?

Because it is a disgrace to the Jews that throughout the forty years of their sojourn in the desert, they only brought this one paschal offering.

TEXT 9

RABBI YEHUDAH LOEW, *GUR ARYEH*, NUMBERS 9:1

שאף אם הוא פטור מן המצוה – או מחמת אונסו או שפטרו – גנאי הוא לו . . . דלא אמרינן "אונס רחמנא פטריה" (בבא קמא כח, ב) רק לענין פטור מן העונש, אבל מכל מקום גנאי הוא לו שלא עשה המצוה, והיה לו זכות. וכאן לא היה להם זכות אותו המצוה . . .

ולא דמי לתרומה וכל המצות התלויות בארץ, דלא חלה המצוה עליהם לגמרי עד שבאו לארץ, אבל פסח שעשו כבר בשנה שנייה, רק שהיו פטורין ממנו עד שבאו לארץ, גנאי להם זה, שדבר זה נקרא שהיו חסרים מצוה.

Rabbi Yehudah Loew (Maharal of Prague)
1525–1609

Talmudist and philosopher. Maharal rose to prominence as leader of the famed Jewish community of Prague. He is the author of more than a dozen works of original philosophic thought, including *Tiferet Yisrael* and *Netzach Yisrael*. He also authored *Gur Aryeh*, a supercommentary to Rashi's biblical commentary; and a commentary on the nonlegal passages of the Talmud. He is buried in the Old Jewish Cemetery of Prague.

An exemption from a mitzvah is not equivalent to doing a mitzvah. . . . When we say, "One who is unable is exempted by G-d" (Bava Kama 28b), we mean that there is no punishment. Nevertheless, it is not the same as doing the mitzvah and receiving the merit. Here too, [though they were exempt,] it was a missed opportunity. . . .

The paschal lamb is different from all the other commandments that were not obligatory in the desert. Those commandments were only activated when they entered Israel. The paschal offering had already been offered in the desert once before, and the Jews were exempted in the ensuing years. Therefore, missing out on this mitzvah is considered a loss despite the exemption.

The Disgrace

TEXT 10

THE REBBE, RABBI MENACHEM MENDEL SCHNEERSON,
LIKUTEI SICHOT 23, PP. 69–70

ווערט די שאלה - ואפילו ביי א בן חמש למקרא: ווי קומט עס אז די אלע ל"ט שנה וואס אידן זיינען געווען אין מדבר האבן זיי ניט געפאדערט און געבעטן פון אויבערשטן "למה נגרע", אז זיי ווילן מקריב זיין דעם "קרבן לה'", דעם קרבן פסח (ובפרט אז דאס איז געווען דער קרבן וואס האט זיי געראטעוועט אין מצרים און געבראכט צו דער גאולה פון מצרים)?

ובמכל שכן וקל וחומר: מה דאך בשעת איינציקע אידן האבן גע'טענה'ט "למה נגרע" האט דער אויבערשטער זיי געגעבן א געלעגנהייט צו מקריב זיין דעם קרבן, על אחת כמה וכמה ווען אלע אידן . . . וואלטן געבעטן און געמאנט ביים אויבערשטן אז זיי ווילן מקריב זיין דעם קרבן פסח בדוגמא ווי זיי האבן דאס געטאן במדבר בשנה השנית, וואלטן זיי דאס אויסגעפירט.

און דאס איז "גנותן של ישראל, שכל ארבעים שנה שהיו ישראל במדבר לא הקריבו אלא פסח זה בלבד" – ווען אידן בעטן ביים אויבערשטן "למה נגרע" וואלטן זיי געפועלט און מקריב געווען דעם קרבן כל ארבעים שנה.

Even a child wonders why the Jews didn't demand the paschal offering during their thirty-nine [subsequent] years in the desert: "Why should we lose out"? [Why did they not tell G-d] that they wanted to bring a paschal offering? (Especially since they knew that this offering saved them in Egypt and brought about their redemption.)

When a mere handful of Jews demanded, "Why should we lose out?" G-d granted them the opportunity to bring the paschal offering. If all the Jews would have pleaded for an opportunity to bring the paschal offering, G-d would surely have consented.

It was, therefore, disgraceful that "throughout the forty years of their sojourn in the desert, they only brought this one paschal offering." Had they demanded of G-d, "Why should we lose out?" they surely would have succeeded and been permitted to bring the paschal offering during those forty years.

III. TRUE LEADERSHIP

Where Was Moses?

TEXT 11

THE REBBE, RABBI MENACHEM MENDEL SCHNEERSON, IBID., P. 70

נשיאי ישראל איז לכל לראש וכל ענינם טראכטן און טאן וועגן אידן. ביז ווי מ׳געפינט בא משה׳ן אז ער האט זיך מוסר נפש געווען פאר כלל ישראל, ניט נאר מסירת הגוף נאר אויך מסירת הנפש, ווי ער האט געזאגט "ואם אין מחני נא מספרך אשר כתבת" (שמות לב, לב).

Jewish leaders are primarily and completely invested in thinking about the people and doing things for the people. Moses even risked his life for the Jewish people. He didn't merely risk his bodily life; he also risked his spiritual life. He said to G-d, "If you don't forgive the Jewish people, erase me from Your book that You wrote" (Exodus 32:32).

TEXT 12

THE REBBE, RABBI MENACHEM MENDEL SCHNEERSON, *LIKUTEI SICHOT*, IBID.

ווען משה ואהרן וואלטן געבעטן ביים אויבערשטן אז זיי זאלן מקריב זיין דעם קרבן פסח, און וואלטן דאס גע'פועל'ט (ואפילו - פאר אלע אידן), וואלט דאס גופא ארויסגעבראכט "גנותן של ישראל" נאך אין א גרעסערן אופן, באווייזנדיק אז דאס איז א קרבן לה' וואס מ'קען פועל זיין הקרבתו דורך בקשה לה' – און אף על פי כן האבן דאס אידן ניט געבעטן.

איז דעריבער האבן משה ואהרן, זייענדיק רועים נאמנים, כדי ניט צו ארויסברענגען (מער בגלוי) "גנותן של ישראל", האבן זיי מוותר געווען אויף זייער עילוי (אין וועלכן זיי זיינען ניט נצטוו געווארן) צו ברענגען א קרבן פסח, דורך בעטן דאס – אבי צו אפהיטן כבודן של ישראל.

Had Moses and Aaron pleaded for the privilege of offering the paschal lamb, it would have been granted to them (and to all the Jews). However, this would have compounded the disgrace of the Jewish people. It would have demonstrated that the Jews could have secured the privilege of this offering with a simple request, but didn't.

To preserve the people's dignity, these faithful shepherds forwent the spiritual gain they could have accrued by pleading for, and bringing, the [non-obligatory] offering.

The Rebbetzin's Statement

TEXT 13

NATHAN LEWIN, *MY FATHER BELONGED TO CHASSIDIM*, LIVING TORAH 120

[The lawyers asked,] "Didn't your father own things? . . . His library and his books, weren't they his personal property?"

She said, "No."

Surprised, they said, "What do you mean [when you say] no? Didn't the Rebbe have personal property?"

She responded, "No. My father, the Rebbe, was the property of Chabad. He belonged to Chabad, and [there was] nothing that he had himself personally."

Nathan Lewin
1936–

Attorney. Born in Lodz, Poland to a distinguished rabbinical family, Nathan Lewin and his family fled the Nazi invasion and arrived in the U.S. in 1941. A graduate of Harvard Law School, Lewin is the founder of Lewin & Lewin LLP and has argued many cases before the Supreme Court of the United States. He is best known for his advocacy for First-Amendment rights and civil liberties, arguing many cases of interest to the American Jewish community.

Moses Desires Israel

TEXT 14

TALMUD, SOTAH 14A

דרש רבי שמלאי: מפני מה נתאוה משה רבינו ליכנס לארץ ישראל? וכי לאכול מפריה הוא צריך, או לשבוע מטובה הוא צריך?

אלא כך אמר משה: הרבה מצות נצטוו ישראל ואין מתקיימין אלא בארץ ישראל. אכנס אני לארץ כדי שיתקיימו כולן על ידי.

Rabbi Simlai expounded, "Why did our teacher Moses desire to enter Israel? Was he desirous of its fruit or its bounty?

"No. Rather this is what Moses was thinking: 'The Jews were given many commandments that can only be fulfilled in Israel. I want to enter the Land and fulfill them all.'"

Babylonian Talmud

A literary work of monumental proportions that draws upon the legal, spiritual, intellectual, ethical, and historical traditions of Judaism. The 37 tractates of the Babylonian Talmud contain the teachings of the Jewish sages from the period after the destruction of the 2nd Temple through the 5th century CE. It has served as the primary vehicle for the transmission of the Oral Law and the education of Jews over the centuries; it is the entry point for all subsequent legal, ethical, and theological Jewish scholarship.

TEXT 15A

MIDRASH, *BAMIDBAR RABAH* 19:13

אמר לו הקדוש ברוך הוא למשה: באיזה פנים אתה מבקש ליכנס לארץ?

משל לרועה שיצא לרעות צאנו של מלך ונשבית הצאן, ביקש הרועה ליכנס לפלטרין של מלך. אמר לו המלך: אם אתה נכנס עכשיו, מה יאמרו הבריות? שאתה השבית הצאן.

אף כאן, אמר לו הקדוש ברוך הוא למשה: שבחך הוא שהוצאת ששים רבוא וקברתם במדבר, ואתה מכניס דור אחר? עכשיו יאמרו, אין לדור המדבר חלק לעולם הבא! אלא תהא בצדן ותבא עמהן . . .

לכך כתיב: "לא תביא את הקהל הזה" (במדבר כ, יב), אלא שיצא עמך.

G-d said to Moses, "How can you desire to enter Israel?"

This can be compared to a shepherd who led the king's flock to the grazing ground and the flock was captured. When the shepherd sought to enter the palace, he was denied entry. The king explained, "If you enter now, what will people think? That you stole the sheep."

Here too, G-d said to Moses, "Is it praiseworthy to lead six-hundred-thousand Jews from captivity in Egypt, bury them all in the desert, and then lead a new generation into Israel? People will say that the generation that was buried in the desert has no share in the World to Come. Rather, remain by their side and be buried with them, and only enter with them when they will enter in the future." . . .

Scripture therefore states, "You will not bring this congregation" (Numbers 20:12), [meaning] rather, you will lead the congregation that emerged from Egypt with you.

Bamidbar Rabah

An exegetical commentary on the first seven chapters of the Book of Numbers and a homiletic commentary on the rest of the book. The first part of *Bamidbar Rabah* is notable for its inclusion of esoteric material; the second half is essentially identical to *Midrash Tanchuma* on the Book of Numbers. It was first printed in Constantinople in 1512, together with four other Midrashic works on the other four books of the Pentateuch.

TEXT 15B

MIDRASH, *DEVARIM RABAH* 7:10

רבונו של עולם, ימות משה ומאה כיוצא בו ולא תנזק צפורנו של אחד מהם.

Dear G-d, may Moses and a hundred like him die, rather than harm a single toenail of the people.

Devarim Rabah

A homiletic commentary on the Book of Deuteronomy. It was first printed in Constantinople in 1512, with four other Midrashic works on the other four books of the Pentateuch. The homilies are structured similarly: each episode begins with a question of religious law and is followed by an answer, which opens with the words, "Our sages taught." Most commentaries end with reassurances and promises of the Redemption.

KEY POINTS

» Bringing the paschal offering in the desert was a dramatic love story between G-d and the Jewish people.

» It also highlighted the disgrace of the Jews, for they never brought another paschal offering in the desert.

» Though they were not instructed to bring the paschal offering, it would most likely have been permitted had they asked.

» Moses and Aaron would have asked for the opportunity, but they held back because that would amplify the disgrace of the people.

» True leaders belong to the people. They never entertain bonus opportunities for personal growth that come at a cost to the people.

9.

Shelach

To Commit, To Question, or . . . Both?

A License to Question Isn't a License to Reject

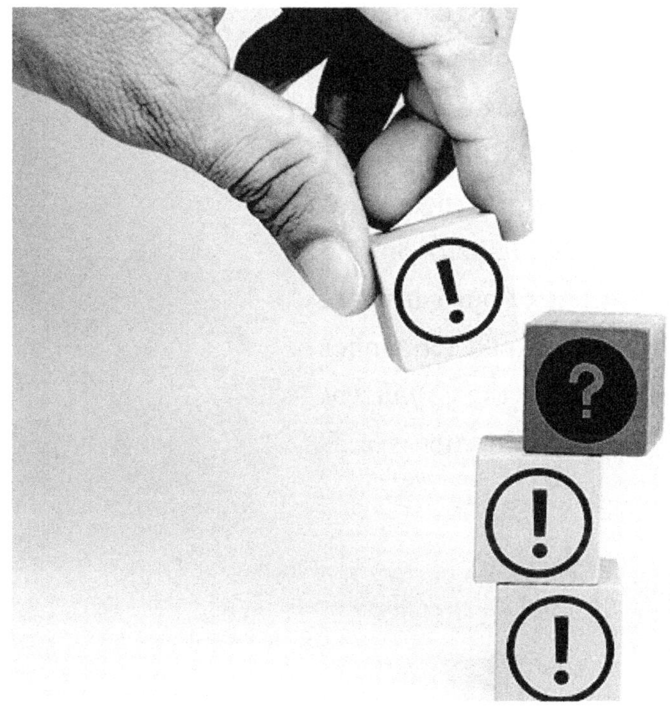

Dedicated in loving memory of Chava bat Moshe,
חוה בת משה,
marking her yahrtzeit *on 21 Sivan.*

May the merit of the Torah study worldwide accompany her soul in the world of everlasting life and be a source of blessings to her family, with much health, happiness, nachas, *and success.*

PARSHAH OVERVIEW

Shelach

Moses sends twelve spies to the land of Canaan. Forty days later they return, carrying a huge cluster of grapes, a pomegranate, and a fig, to report on a lush and bountiful land. But ten of the spies warn that the inhabitants of the land are giants and warriors "more powerful than we"; only Caleb and Joshua insist that the land can be conquered, as G-d has commanded.

The people weep that they'd rather return to Egypt. G-d decrees that Israel's entry into the land shall be delayed forty years, during which time that entire generation will die out in the desert. A group of remorseful Jews storm the mountain on the border of the land, and are routed by the Amalekites and Canaanites. The laws of the *menachot* (meal, wine, and oil offerings) are given, as well as the mitzvah to consecrate a portion of the dough *(challah)* to G-d when making bread. A man violates the Shabbat by gathering sticks, and he is put to death. G-d instructs us to place fringes *(tzitzit)* on the four corners of our garments so that we should remember to fulfill the *mitzvot* (Divine commandments).

I. ENIGMATIC INSTRUCTIONS

A Clandestine Mission

TEXT 1

DEUTERONOMY 1:22

וַתִּקְרְבוּן אֵלַי כֻּלְּכֶם וַתֹּאמְרוּ, נִשְׁלְחָה אֲנָשִׁים לְפָנֵינוּ וְיַחְפְּרוּ לָנוּ אֶת הָאָרֶץ, וְיָשִׁבוּ אֹתָנוּ דָּבָר אֶת הַדֶּרֶךְ אֲשֶׁר נַעֲלֶה בָּהּ וְאֵת הֶעָרִים אֲשֶׁר נָבֹא אֲלֵיהֶן:

You all approached me and said, "Let's send men to search out the land and bring back word about which route we should ascend, and which cities we should enter."

TEXT 2A

NUMBERS 13:2

שְׁלַח לְךָ אֲנָשִׁים, וְיָתֻרוּ אֶת אֶרֶץ כְּנַעַן אֲשֶׁר אֲנִי נֹתֵן לִבְנֵי יִשְׂרָאֵל:

Send out men for yourself to scout the land of Canaan that I am giving to the Jews.

Ambiguous Response

TEXT 2B

RASHI, AD LOC.

"שלח לך": לדעתך, אני איני מצוה לך, אם תרצה שלח.

Send for yourself: As you understand. I am not telling you to send. If you want to send, send.

Rabbi Shlomo Yitzchaki (Rashi)
1040–1105

Most noted biblical and Talmudic commentator. Born in Troyes, France, Rashi studied in the famed *yeshivot* of Mainz and Worms. His commentaries on the Pentateuch and the Talmud, which focus on the straightforward meaning of the text, appear in virtually every edition of the Talmud and Bible.

Gargantuan Grapes

TEXT 3A

NUMBERS 13:20

וּמָה הָאָרֶץ, הַשְּׁמֵנָה הִוא אִם רָזָה, הֲיֵשׁ בָּהּ עֵץ אִם אַיִן, וְהִתְחַזַּקְתֶּם
וּלְקַחְתֶּם מִפְּרִי הָאָרֶץ:

What is the nature of the soil—is it fat or lean? Are there trees or not? Gird yourselves and take from the fruit of the land.

Betting the Entire House

TEXT 3B

NACHMANIDES, AD LOC.

וטעם "והתחזקתם ולקחתם", שלא יפחדו בלקחם מפרי הארץ פן יכירו בהם שהם מרגלים.

"Gird yourselves with courage and take fruit." Don't be afraid that if you take fruit from the land, you might be exposed as spies.

Rabbi Moshe ben Nachman (Nachmanides, Ramban)
1194–1270

Scholar, philosopher, author, and physician. Nachmanides was born in Spain and served as leader of Iberian Jewry. In 1263, he was summoned by King James of Aragon to a public disputation with Pablo Cristiani, a Jewish apostate. Though Nachmanides was the clear victor of the debate, he had to flee Spain because of the resulting persecution. He moved to Israel and helped reestablish communal life in Jerusalem. He authored a classic commentary on the Pentateuch and a commentary on the Talmud.

II. LICENSE TO ASK

The Core Root Approach

TEXT 4

RABBI YEHUDAH ARYEH LEIB ALTER, *SEFAT EMET*, SHEMINI 5659

דעיקר עשיות המצוה בכח הציווי, וזה למעלה מכל הכוונות.

שהרי נדב ואביהוא, שהיו גדולי עולם והיה להם כוונות ויחודים וסודות במעשיהם, אף על פי כן, מצד שלא צוה אותם נענשו.

קל וחומר מדה טובה המרובה, המקיים המצוה לעשות ציווי הבורא אף על פי שאינו יודע כלום, חשוב ככל הכוונות.

The primary reason to perform a mitzvah is that G-d commanded it. This is greater than all other intentions.

Nadab and Abihu, some of the greatest Jews of their time, had many lofty intentions. Yet they were punished for doing something that they were not instructed to do.

When applied to the positive, this principle is even more compelling. It tells us that simply performing a mitzvah with no understanding—purely out of obedience to G-d—is loftier than all sacred intentions.

Rabbi Yehudah Aryeh Leib Alter (*Sefat Emet*) 1847–1905

Chasidic master and scholar. Rabbi Yehudah Aryeh Leib Alter assumed the leadership of the Chasidic dynasty of Gur (Gora), a town near Warsaw, Poland, at the age of 23. He was the grandson and successor of Rabbi Yitzchak Meir of Gur, the founder of the Gur dynasty. He is commonly referred to as the *Sefat Emet*, after the title of his commentaries on the Torah and Talmud.

TEXT 5A

MAIMONIDES, *MISHNEH TORAH*, LAWS OF SUBSTITUTES 4:13

אַף עַל פִּי שֶׁכָּל חֻקֵּי הַתּוֹרָה גְּזֵרוֹת הֵם . . . רָאוּי לְהִתְבּוֹנֵן בָּהֶן וְכָל מַה שֶּׁאַתָּה יָכוֹל לִתֵּן לוֹ טַעַם, תֵּן לוֹ טַעַם. הֲרֵי אָמְרוּ חֲכָמִים הָרִאשׁוֹנִים שֶׁהַמֶּלֶךְ שְׁלֹמֹה הֵבִין רֹב הַטְּעָמִים שֶׁל כָּל חֻקֵּי הַתּוֹרָה.

Although all of the Torah's statutes are suprarational decrees, . . . it is appropriate to meditate upon them and, wherever possible, provide a reason. The sages of the early generations said that King Solomon understood most of the rationales for all of the statutes of the Torah.

Rabbi Moshe ben Maimon (Maimonides, Rambam)
1135–1204

Halachist, philosopher, author, and physician. Maimonides was born in Córdoba, Spain. After the conquest of Córdoba by the Almohads, he fled Spain and eventually settled in Cairo, Egypt. There, he became the leader of the Jewish community and served as court physician to the vizier of Egypt. He is most noted for authoring the *Mishneh Torah*, an encyclopedic arrangement of Jewish law; and for his philosophical work, *Guide for the Perplexed*. His rulings on Jewish law are integral to the formation of Halachic consensus.

TEXT 5B

RABBI SHLOMO AVINER, *SEFER HAKUZARI PIRUSH* 2:28, P. 219

מסופר (במסכת שבת י, א): רבי ירמיה היה יושב לפני רבי זירא ולומד תורה. הגיע זמן מנחה ורבי ירמיה היה בהול לסיים את לימודו שלא יאחר לתפילה. קרא עליו רבי זירא את הפסוק: "מסיר אוזנו משמע תורה גם תפילתו תועבה" (משלי כח, ט).

אם אינך לומד כראוי, גם תפילתך, תהא מכוונת ככל שתהא, היא תועבה. אמנם אתה מתפלל אל ה' בכל לבבך, אלא אינך יודע כראוי מיהו וכיצד עובדים אותו.

The Talmud (Shabbat 10a) relates that Rabbi Yirmiyah was sitting before Rabbi Zeira and studying Torah. The time for the afternoon prayer service had arrived, and Rabbi Yirmiyah hurried to complete his studies. When Rabbi Zeira saw this, he proclaimed, "One who turns his ear from hearing the Torah, his prayer is also an abomination" (Proverbs 28:9).

If you don't study the Torah appropriately, no matter how mindful you are during prayer, your prayer is abominable. You might pray to G-d with all your heart, but you won't know who G-d is and how to worship Him properly.

Rabbi Shlomo Aviner
1943–

Rabbi and author. Born and raised in France, Rabbi Aviner made *aliyah* to Israel and studied in Yeshivat Merkaz HaRav, where he became a close disciple of Rabbi Tzvi Yehudah Kook, the ideological leader of the Religious Zionist movement. Rabbi Aviner serves as the Rabbi of Bet El and the head of Yeshivat Ateret Yerushalayim in the Old City of Jerusalem. He is the author of dozens of books, including Halachic responsa and commentaries on the philosophical writings of Rabbi Avraham Yitzchak Kook.

G-d Wants the Mind

TEXT 6A

RABBI SHNEUR ZALMAN OF LIADI, *LIKUTEI AMARIM*, CH. 38

שֶׁזֶּהוּ גַם כֵּן רְצוֹנוֹ יִתְבָּרֵךְ, לְדָבְקָה בְּשֵׂכֶל וּמַחֲשָׁבָה, וְכַוָּנַת הַמִּצְוֹת מַעֲשִׂיּוֹת, וּבְכַוָּנַת קְרִיאַת שְׁמַע וּתְפִלָּה וּשְׁאָר בְּרָכוֹת.

וְהֶאָרַת רָצוֹן הָעֶלְיוֹן הַזֶּה הַמְּאִירָה וּמְלוּבֶּשֶׁת בְּכַוָּנָה זוֹ הִיא גְדוֹלָה לְאֵין קֵץ, לְמַעְלָה מַעְלָה מֵהֶאָרַת רָצוֹן הָעֶלְיוֹן הַמְּאִירָה וּמְלוּבֶּשֶׁת בְּקִיּוּם הַמִּצְוֹת עַצְמָן בְּמַעֲשֶׂה וּבְדִבּוּר בְּלִי כַוָּנָה.

This too is G-d's will. G-d wants us to bind our minds and thoughts to Him. He wants us to be mindful as we fulfill His commandments, recite the Shema, pray, and chant the blessings.

When we use our minds, the degree of Divinity we channel is immeasurably greater than the Divine will channeled by a mindless fulfillment of His will, utilizing only our actions and/or words.

Rabbi Shneur Zalman of Liadi (Alter Rebbe)
1745–1812

Chasidic rebbe, Halachic authority, and founder of the Chabad movement. The Alter Rebbe was born in Liozna, Belarus, and was among the principal students of the Magid of Mezeritch. His numerous works include the *Tanya*, an early classic containing the fundamentals of Chabad Chasidism; and *Shulchan Aruch HaRav*, an expanded and reworked code of Jewish law.

G-d Wants the Heart

TEXT 6B

ISAIAH 29:13

כִּי נִגַּשׁ הָעָם הַזֶּה בְּפִיו, וּבִשְׂפָתָיו כִּבְּדוּנִי, וְלִבּוֹ רִחַק מִמֶּנִּי. וַתְּהִי יִרְאָתָם אֹתִי מִצְוַת אֲנָשִׁים מְלֻמָּדָה:

The people approach me with their mouths and honor me with their lips, but their hearts are distant from me. They obey me by rote.

Isaiah

Biblical book. The book of Isaiah contains the prophecies of Isaiah, who lived in the 7th–6th centuries BCE. Isaiah's prophecies contain stern rebukes for the personal failings of the contemporary people of Judea and the corruption of its government. The bulk of the prophecies, however, are stirring consolations and poetic visions of the future Redemption.

Why and How to Ask

TEXT 7

RABBI LORD JONATHAN SACKS, *RABBI JONATHAN SACKS'S HAGGADAH: HEBREW AND ENGLISH TEXT WITH NEW ESSAYS AND COMMENTARY* (JERUSALEM: MAGGID BOOKS, 2015), PP. 106–108

There are three conditions, though, for asking a Jewish question.

The first is that we seek genuinely to learn—not to doubt, ridicule, dismiss, reject. That is what the 'wicked son' of the Haggadah does: ask not out of a desire to understand but as a prelude to walking away.

Second is that we accept limits to our understanding. Not everything is intelligible at any given moment. There were scientists at the beginning of the twentieth century who believed that virtually every major discovery had already been made—not suspecting that the next hundred years would give rise to Einstein's relativity theory, Heisenberg's uncertainty principle, Gödel's theorem, proof of the 'Big Bang' origin of the universe, the discovery of DNA and the decoding of the human genome.

In relation to Torah, there were many German and American Jews in the nineteenth century who could not understand Jewish prayers for a return to Zion, and deleted them from the prayer book.

These facts should induce in us a certain humility. Not every scientific orthodoxy survives the test of time. Not everything in Judaism that we do not understand is unintelligible. The very features of Jewish life one generation finds difficult, the next generation may find the most meaningful of all. Faith is not opposed to questions, but it is opposed to the shallow certainty that what we understand is all there is.

Rabbi Lord Jonathan Sacks
1948–2020

Chief Rabbi of the United Kingdom from 1991 through 2013. Rabbi Sacks attended Cambridge University and received his doctorate from King's College, London. A prolific and influential author, his books include *Will We Have Jewish Grandchildren?* and *The Dignity of Difference.* He received the Jerusalem Prize in 1995 for his contributions to enhancing Jewish life in the Diaspora, was knighted and made a life peer in 2005, and became Baron Sacks of Aldridge in 2009.

Third is that when it comes to Torah, we learn by living and understand by doing. We learn to understand music by listening to music. We learn to appreciate literature by reading literature. There is no way of understanding Shabbat without keeping Shabbat, no way of appreciating how Jewish laws of family purity enhance a marriage without observing them. Judaism, like music, is something that can only be understood from the inside, by immersing yourself in it.

Given these caveats, Judaism is a faith that, more than any other, values the mind, encouraging questions and engaging us at the highest level of intellectual rigor. Every question asked in reverence is the start of a journey towards G-d.

TEXT 8A

RASHI, GENESIS 6:6

אפיקורוס אחד שאל את רבי יהושע בן קרחה. אמר לו: "אין אתם מודים שהקדוש ברוך הוא רואה את הנולד?"

אמר לו: "הן".

אמר לו: "והא כתיב, 'ויתעצב אל לבו'" (בראשית ה, ו)?

אמר לו: "נולד לך בן זכר מימיך?"

אמר לו: "הן".

אמר לו: "ומה עשית?"

אמר לו: "שמחתי ושימחתי את הכל".

אמר לו: "ולא היית יודע שסופו למות?"

אמר לו: "בשעת חדותא חדותא, בשעת אבלא אבלא".

אמר לו: "כך מעשה הקדוש ברוך הוא. אף על פי שגלוי לפניו שסופן לחטוא ולאבדן, לא נמנע מלבראן בשביל הצדיקים העתידים לעמוד מהם".

A heretic asked Rabbi Yehoshua ben Korchah, "Do you not admit that G-d foresees the future?"

Rabbi Yehoshua replied, "Yes."

The heretic retorted, "But the passage states, 'And He became grieved in His heart'" (Genesis 5:6).

Rabbi Yehoshua replied, "Was a son ever born to you?"

"Yes."

"And what did you do?"

"I rejoiced and ensured that everyone else rejoiced as well."

"But did you not know that he was destined to die?"

"At the time of joy, joy; at the time of mourning, mourning."

Rabbi Yehoshua replied, "So is it with G-d. Though He knew that the people would sin, and that He would destroy them, He created them for the sake of the righteous people who would arise from them."

TEXT 8B

THE REBBE, RABBI MENACHEM MENDEL SCHNEERSON,
TORAT MENACHEM 5751:1, P. 201

סגנון שאלתו של אפיקורוס - "אי אתם מודים שהקדוש ברוך הוא רואה את הנולד . . . והא כתיב ויתעצב אל לבו" (בראשית ה, ו) - היא באופן של אפיקורסות, ש"מוכיח" ממה שכתוב "ויתעצב אל לבו" שאי אפשר לומר שהקדוש ברוך הוא רואה את הנולד.

אבל ילד יהודי שואל בסגנון הפוך: ברור ומוחלט אצלו בוודאות גמורה שהתורה היא אמת, משה אמת ותורתו אמת. וברור אצלו ללא כל ספק שהקדוש ברוך הוא רואה את הנולד וכו', אלא שרוצה להבין (בשכלו) מהי ההסברה בשינוי מחשבתו של הקדוש ברוך הוא, מהי הסיבה שהביאה לשינוי מחשבתו של שהקדוש ברוך הוא, וכיוצא בזה.

Rabbi Menachem Mendel Schneerson
1902–1994

The towering Jewish leader of the 20th century, known as "the Lubavitcher Rebbe," or simply as "the Rebbe." Born in southern Ukraine, the Rebbe escaped Nazi-occupied Europe, arriving in the U.S. in June 1941. The Rebbe inspired and guided the revival of traditional Judaism after the European devastation, impacting virtually every Jewish community the world over. The Rebbe often emphasized that the performance of just one additional good deed could usher in the era of Mashiach. The Rebbe's scholarly talks and writings have been printed in more than 200 volumes.

The heretic asks questions in a heretical style: "How can you believe that G-d foreknows the future if the passage states, 'He became grieved in His heart'" (Genesis 5:6)? His point is that it is impossible to believe that G-d knows the future.

A Jew asks the same question, but in the opposite manner. We ae absolutely certain that the Torah is true, that G-d foresees the future, etc. However, we seek to understand how there can be a change or what causes change in G-d's mind, etc.

III. DO YOU UNDERSTAND?

Their Choice

TEXT 9A

THE REBBE, RABBI MENACHEM MENDEL SCHNEERSON,
LIKUTEI SICHOT 23, PP. 93–94

דער טעם פארוואס דער אויבערשטער האט ניט אנגעזאגט אויף שילוח המרגלים, נאר "שלח לך - לדעתך":

היות אז דער מכוון פון שילוח המרגלים איז צו אויפטאן ביי אידן דעם "נשמע" בנוגע דער כניסה לארץ, איז דעריבער אויך דער שילוח גופא געקומען אין אן אופן פון "לדעתך" - אז מען טוט עס ווייל אזוי דארף זיין מצד דעת (און ניט בלויז אין אן אופן פון "נעשה", ווייל "אני מצוה לך").

The reason G-d left the decision to Moses with"If you want to send, send":

The purpose of sending the spies was to activate the "we will listen" dimension of Judaism—enabling the people to understand how they would conquer Israel. Therefore, the dispatch itself had to come from them: "If you want to send, send." It had to be done because *they* felt it necessary to send spies, not because G-d instructed it.

Seeing and Hearing

TEXT 9B

THE REBBE, RABBI MENACHEM MENDEL SCHNEERSON, IBID.

דער אויבערשטער האט טאקע געזאגט אידן אז זי איז אן ארץ טובה ורחבה גו' - אבער דער אויבערשטער וויל אז אידן זאלן איינזען דעם גוטס פון ארץ ישראל אויך בשכלם הם.

און דעריבער האט משה רבינו געהייסן ברענגען מפרי הארץ, כדי אז דער רצון פון אידן צו גיין קיין ארץ ישראל זאל זיין (ניט נאר ווייל אזוי האט דער אויבערשטער געהייסן ובמילא פאלגן זיי דעם ציווי ה' (נעשה) – נאר) אויך מצד זיי אליין, זיי פארשטייען אז מ'דארף ווען גיין קיין ארץ ישראל, ווייל זי איז די אמת'ע ארץ טובה ורחבה.

G-d had indeed informed the Jews that Israel is a good and prosperous land, but G-d wanted the Jews to understand this truth on their own.

Moses, therefore, instructed the spies to bring back some of the fruit. When the people would behold the fruit, they would surmise that it is truly a good and prosperous land. Their desire for Israel would be kindled, not because G-d had instructed it and they had pledged to obey Him, but because they would truly want to go.

No Gain without Pain

TEXT 9C

THE REBBE, RABBI MENACHEM MENDEL SCHNEERSON, IBID.

און די זעלבע זאך איז בנוגע דעם (ערשטן) טייל פון זייער שליחות - צו אויסגעפינען אין וועלכן וועג מ'זאל כובש זיין ארץ ישראל, אז די כוונה דערביי איז געווען אז אידן זאלן איינזען בשכלם ווי "יכול נוכל לה".

The same applies to the first part of their mission—to discover the surest methods to conquer Israel. G-d's purpose was to enable the Jews to understand, not just to be told, that the land could be conquered.

TEXT 10

THE REBBE, RABBI MENACHEM MENDEL SCHNEERSON,
SEFER HASICHOT 5749:2, P. 538

לא זו בלבד שמשה לא חשש שיש כאן ענין בלתי רצוי אלא אדרבה היה שמח על החידוש שבדיבור זה. שעבודת המטה תוכל להיות באופן של בחירה חפשית לגמרי ללא ההכרח דציווי הקדוש ברוך הוא כי אם מדעתו ומרצונו של האדם. שיהיו מתאימים מעצמם לרצונו של הקדוש ברוך הוא.

Not only was Moses unconcerned that G-d's ambiguous response portended a negative outcome, he was elated over the new opportunity. Jews would now be empowered to serve G-d because they chose to rather than because they felt compelled by G-d's instructions. To do what G-d wants because they understand it to be good and want to do it. To be spontaneously synchronized with G-d's will.

KEY POINTS

- The foundation of Judaism is to accept the truth of G-d and to obey Him without thinking.
- The ultimate form of Judaism is to probe, ask, and understand so that our minds and hearts are aligned with G-d's thoughts and wishes.
- The license to think is not a license to reject, but there is a risk that some might take it that way.
- To avoid this, it helps to remember that we don't ask to satisfy our curiosity, but because G-d wants us to connect with Him through our minds and hearts.
- This shapes the way we formulate our questions. Rather than questioning the Torah's truth, we seek to understand it. If we fail, we don't reject. We simply keep looking.
- Sending the spies was the first experiment with independent thought. Although the spies misused their license, we learn from their mistakes and get it right.

10.

Korach

Power to the Little Guy

Why Judaism Cherishes Ordinary People over Holy Saints

Dedicated to Peter and Hazel Pflaum, in appreciation of their friendship and partnership with JLI and their dedication to bringing the light of Torah to communities across the globe.

PARSHAH OVERVIEW

Korach

Korah incites a mutiny, challenging Moses's leadership and the granting of the *kehunah* (priesthood) to Aaron. He is accompanied by Moses's inveterate foes, Dathan and Abiram. Joining them are 250 distinguished members of the community, who offer the sacrosanct *ketoret* (incense) to prove their worthiness for the priesthood. The earth opens up and swallows the mutineers, and a fire consumes the *ketoret* offerers.

A subsequent plague is stopped by Aaron's offering of *ketoret*. Aaron's staff miraculously blossoms and brings forth almonds to prove that his designation as High Priest is Divinely ordained.

G-d commands that a *terumah* ("uplifting") offering be given to the *Kohanim* (priests) from each crop of grain, wine, and oil; as well as from all firstborn sheep and cattle, and other specified gifts.

I. A REBELLION OVERCOME

The Tactic

TEXT 1

RASHI, NUMBERS 16:1

ויקח קרח: לקח את עצמו לצד אחד להיות נחלק מתוך העדה לעורר על הכהונה.

וזהו שתרגם אונקלוס "ואתפלג", נחלק משאר העדה להחזיק במחלוקת.

"And Korah took." He took himself to one side to be separated from the congregation to challenge the priesthood.

Unkelos [the classic translator of the Torah into Aramaic] thus translated "he took" as, "he split." He split from the congregation to create divisiveness.

Rabbi Shlomo Yitzchaki (Rashi)
1040–1105

Most noted biblical and Talmudic commentator. Born in Troyes, France, Rashi studied in the famed *yeshivot* of Mainz and Worms. His commentaries on the Pentateuch and the Talmud, which focus on the straightforward meaning of the text, appear in virtually every edition of the Talmud and Bible.

The Motive

TEXT 2

NUMBERS 16:3

וַיִּקָּהֲלוּ עַל מֹשֶׁה וְעַל אַהֲרֹן וַיֹּאמְרוּ אֲלֵהֶם רַב לָכֶם, כִּי כָל הָעֵדָה כֻּלָּם קְדֹשִׁים וּבְתוֹכָם ה', וּמַדּוּעַ תִּתְנַשְּׂאוּ עַל קְהַל ה'?

[Korah's group] gathered against Moses and Aaron and said to them, "You take too much for yourselves. The entire nation is holy, and G-d is among them, so why do you raise yourselves over G-d's people?"

TEXT 3

THE REBBE, RABBI MENACHEM MENDEL SCHNEERSON,
LIKUTEI SICHOT 18, PP. 219–220

וויבאלד אז א כהן איז אינגאנצן אפגעשיידט פון עניני העולם, ער איז פארנומען נאר מיט קדושה זאכן - ובלשון הכתוב "ויבדל אהרן להקדישו קודש קדשים הוא ובניו" (דברי הימים א כג, יג), ובפרט (אהרן) א כהן גדול אויך ווענען עס שטייט "ומן המקדש לא יצא" (ויקרא כא, יב).

איז "מדוע תתנשאו על קהל ה'" (במדבר טז, ג) – הייסט ווי אזוי און פארוואס דארף זיין די השפעה פון דער התנשאות וקדושת אהרון אויף אידן (על קהל ה'), אז אויך זיי זאלן זיך אויפהויבן צו זיין מובדל פון עניני העולם, בשעת אז זייער עבודה איז צו פארנעמען זיך מיט דברים גשמיים און מאכן פון זיי כלים צו אלוקות?

The *Kohen* is completely insulated from worldly affairs—exclusively engaged with sacred matters, as the Torah says, "Aaron was separated, consecrated to be holy of holies, he and his sons" (I Chronicles 23:13). This is especially true of Aaron, about whom it is written, "He must not emerge from the Temple" (Leviticus 21:12).

If so, Korah claimed, "Why do you raise yourselves over G-d's people" (Numbers 16:3)? How and why must Aaron's lofty sanctity inspire everyone to be transcendent and to separate from worldly affairs? The people's role is to engage with the world, and to fulfill G-d's wish through this engagement.

Rabbi Menachem Mendel Schneerson
1902–1994

The towering Jewish leader of the 20th century, known as "the Lubavitcher Rebbe," or simply as "the Rebbe." Born in southern Ukraine, the Rebbe escaped Nazi-occupied Europe, arriving in the U.S. in June 1941. The Rebbe inspired and guided the revival of traditional Judaism after the European devastation, impacting virtually every Jewish community the world over. The Rebbe often emphasized that the performance of just one additional good deed could usher in the era of Mashiach. The Rebbe's scholarly talks and writings have been printed in more than 200 volumes.

Priestly Offerings

TEXT 4

NUMBERS 18:19

כֹּל תְּרוּמֹת הַקֳּדָשִׁים אֲשֶׁר יָרִימוּ בְנֵי יִשְׂרָאֵל לַה', נָתַתִּי לְךָ וּלְבָנֶיךָ וְלִבְנֹתֶיךָ.

All the sacred gifts that Jews set aside for G-d, I have given to you, your sons and your daughters.

I. JUDAISM IS A BRIDGE

Fit To Be Tied

TEXT 5

RABBI ABRAHAM SABA, *TZROR HAMOR*, NUMBERS 16:1

סוד הציצית הוא קשור ואחוד בסבת ה' הקדוש. שהוא הקשר המקשר כל הדברים והחוליות בין הקשרים. להורות כי גבוה מעל גבוה שומר וגבוהים עליהם, ועליון יחיד על כולם הנותן קשר לכולם . . .

ולהורות על כל זה צוותה התורה "ונתנו על ציצית הכנף פתיל תכלת", להורות על היחיד עליון הנקרא חוט השני, שהוא ה' המחבר ותופר ומקשר בחוט אחד כל הדברים. והוא א-ל עליון קונה שמים וארץ ומחברם באחדים.

וזה הייחוד והקישור יש לו לכוון לכל איש שנקרא בשם יהודי ולובש טלית זה, שהוא מחובר וקשור נפלא עם ה' אחד. ובזה הוא חלק אדם מא-ל, וחלק אלוקה מעולמו.

The secret of *tzitzit* is to tie and unite ourselves with G-d, the sacred First Cause of existence. G-d is represented by the top knot of the *tzitzit*—the one that binds the disparate pieces and wrappings that are located between the knots. The successive knots of the *tzitzit* demonstrate the many spheres of existence, each higher than the other. The top knot demonstrates that above all is the absolute unity of G-d, Who ties it all together. . . .

Thus, the Torah commands, "Affix a sky-blue thread upon the fringes on the corners" (Numbers 15:38). This teaches us that the Singular Supernal One, who is also described [in kabbalistic works] as the scarlet thread, attaches, sews, and ties everything together with a single thread. He, the Master of Heaven and earth, combines everything and makes them one.

Rabbi Abraham Saba
1440–1508

Bible commentator and preacher. Born in Castile, Spain, Rabbi Abraham Saba was a prolific writer, but his manuscripts were lost as he fled from Spain and Portugal when the Jews were expelled. Settling in *Fes*, Morocco, he reproduced many of his lost works, including his Torah commentary *Tzror Hamor*.

As we wrap ourselves in the fringed prayer shawl, we remember this unifying knot and visualize our wondrous connection and attachment to the One G-d. This way, the human becomes part of G-d and G-d has a presence in His world.

TEXT 6

MIDRASH, *BAMIDBAR RABAH* 18:3

קָפַץ קֹרַח וְאָמַר לְמֹשֶׁה: טַלִּית שֶׁכֻּלָּהּ תְּכֵלֶת, מַהוּ שֶׁתְּהֵא פְּטוּרָה מִן הַצִּיצִית?

אָמַר לוֹ: חַיֶּיבֶת בְּצִיצִית.

אָמַר לוֹ קֹרַח: טַלִּית שֶׁכֻּלָּהּ תְּכֵלֶת אֵין פּוֹטֶרֶת עַצְמָהּ, אַרְבָּעָה חוּטִין פּוֹטְרוֹת אוֹתָהּ?

Korah arose and asked Moses, "Does a prayer shawl made entirely of sky-blue wool require sky-blue fringes on its corners?"

Moses replied, "The fringes are still required."

Korah said, "If an entire sky-blue garment can't exempt one from the obligation, how can four sky-blue fringes exempt us?"

Bamidbar Rabah

An exegetical commentary on the first seven chapters of the book of Numbers and a homiletic commentary on the rest of the book. The first part of *Bamidbar Rabah* is notable for its inclusion of esoteric material; the second half is essentially identical to *Midrash Tanchuma* on the book of Numbers. It was first printed in Constantinople in 1512, together with 4 other Midrashic works on the other 4 books of the Pentateuch.

Korah Missed the Point

TEXT 7

RABBI LORD JONATHAN SACKS, *A JUDAISM ENGAGED WITH THE WORLD* (LONDON, U.K.: EXCO DPS LTD., 2013), PP. 14–15

We are commanded to lead our lives so that we become living tutorials in the values Jews first taught the world: the sanctity of life, the dignity of the human person, the twin imperatives of justice and compassion, marriage as a covenant and the home as a sanctuary, community as collective responsibility, the importance of lifelong education, respect for the elderly, and many other ideals that Jews were the first to embrace and of which they are still the great exemplars.

When Dr. Ludwig Guttmann revolutionized the care of paraplegics and created the Paralympics, that was a Kiddush Hashem. When Viktor Frankl in Auschwitz gave his fellow prisoners the will to live, creating a new psychotherapy based on "man's search for meaning," that was a Kiddush Hashem. When Jewish economists develop ways of alleviating poverty throughout the developing world, that is a Kiddush Hashem. When Jewish businesses set new standards in respecting employees, that is a Kiddush Hashem. When Jews worked with Nelson Mandela to end apartheid or marched with Martin Luther King in the battle for civil rights, that was a Kiddush Hashem.

The reason is that each of these is a way of showing what G-d wants from us in this world. He wants us to become His "partners in the work of Creation." He wants us to fight the evil men do to one another. He wants us to use our freedom responsibly. He wants us to use our G-d-given powers to enhance the lives of others.

Rabbi Lord Jonathan Sacks 1948–2020

Chief Rabbi of the United Kingdom from 1991 through 2013. Rabbi Sacks attended Cambridge University and received his doctorate from King's College, London. A prolific and influential author, his books include *Will We Have Jewish Grandchildren?* and *The Dignity of Difference.* He received the Jerusalem Prize in 1995 for his contributions to enhancing Jewish life in the Diaspora, was knighted and made a life peer in 2005, and became Baron Sacks of Aldridge in 2009.

The Priestly Gift, Not the Sacrifice

TEXT 8

THE REBBE, RABBI MENACHEM MENDEL SCHNEERSON, *LIKUTEI SICHOT* 18, P. 223

אין הקרבת הקרבנות (ובכללות דער ענין פון קדשים, וואס א איד איז מקדיש זיינע נכסים לה') זאגט זיך ניט ארויס אז אלס דברים תחתונים גשמיים ווערען זיי א כלי צו אלוקות, ווארום די קרבנות גייען דאך ארויס פון חול, פון זייער שייכות צום אדם למטה, און ווערן אן ענין קדוש . . .

מה שאין כן בא מתנות כהונה, וואס א מענטש גיט אוועק פון זיין פארמעגען צום כהן . . . דוקא אין דעם איז ניכר ומודגש אז אויך במצבם פון ענינים דלמטה (אלס חולין) זיינען זיי שייך צו אלוקות.

Offering a sacrifice or consecrating any of our possessions to G-d fails to capture the concept of transforming mundane physical items into Divine instruments. They represent the idea of escaping all association with mundane worldliness and becoming sacred.

By contrast, giving our mundane possessions as priestly gifts to the *Kohen* . . . demonstrates the notion that mundane worldly possessions can become holy.

In G-d We Trust

TEXT 9

"THE LEGISLATION PLACING 'IN G-D WE TRUST' ON NATIONAL CURRENCY," WWW.HOUSE.GOV

On this date [July 11, 1955], President Dwight D. Eisenhower signed into law H.R. 619, a bill that required that the inscription "In G-d We Trust" appear on all paper and coin currency.

Representative Charles E. Bennett of Florida introduced the resolution in the House. . . . Adding "In G-d We Trust" to currency, Bennett believed, would "serve as a constant reminder" that the nation's political and economic fortunes were tied to its spiritual faith.

The inscription had appeared on most U.S. coins since the Civil War. . . . However, "In G-d We Trust" had not appeared on paper currency and, from time to time, had not been inscribed on certain classes of coins.

Bennett's measure sailed through the House, passing on an unrecorded voice vote. The Senate approved the measure less than three weeks later. The first dollar bills bearing the inscription entered circulation in 1957, shortly after "In God We Trust" also had been made the official national motto by an act of Congress.

III. THE EXTRAORDINARY ORDINARY JEW

The Reward

TEXT 10

THE REBBE, RABBI MENACHEM MENDEL SCHNEERSON, *LIKUTEI SICHOT* 18, P. 228

אין דעם דוקא דריקט זיך אויס ווי אזוי אויך אזעלכע, וואס זיינען תחתונים אין זייער מציאות הנראית והנגלית זיינען שייך צו אלוקות. אז אין וועלכער מדריגה א איד געפינט זיך נאה, איז זיין אמת'ער און פנימיות'דיקער מציאות – אלוקות.

This truly highlights the fact that even those who seem low on the surface are deeply attached to G-d. No matter their station in life, the true and internal reality of every Jew is G-d.

The Holier Soul

TEXT 11

THE REBBE, RABBI MENACHEM MENDEL SCHNEERSON,
TORAT MENACHEM 5730:1 (58), P. 143

בעלי עסק שיש להם קשיים, יש להם כחות נעלים יותר מאשר יושבי אוהל שאין להם קשיים, כך, שאי אפשר לדעת כיצד היו מתנהגים אילו היה להם קשיים.

ובגלל זה סיבבו מלמעלה שישארו בישיבה או בכולל. ואילו בעלי עסק שיש להם קשיים – הרי זה גופא מוכיח שיש להם כחות על זה.

Jews who live in the world have more spiritual stamina than those who are cloistered in the halls of Torah study. The spiritual integrity of Torah students is never challenged by secularism because they are not exposed to it. We, therefore, don't know how they might fare if they were to be exposed to such challenges.

In fact, it is because they are not gifted with the same spiritual stamina that G-d guided them from Above to a cloistered life in the study hall. Not so the businessperson. The very fact that they face daily challenges indicates that they have the spiritual stamina to overcome these challenges.

KEY POINTS

» Korah thought that holy Jews should live in their cloistered world of prayer and study while ordinary Jews live in the real world: that the two should have little contact.

» Moses and Aaron taught that the role of the holy Jew is to go out into the world and connect the ordinary Jew with G-d: to empower them to be *in* the world but not *of* the world.

» G-d agreed with Moses and demonstrated this through the laws of the priestly gifts. These gifts are made by the ordinary Jew to the priest. The part that is gifted becomes holy; the rest remains in the possession of the giver and remains mundane.

» This blend of holy and mundane represents the Jewish principle that holiness and mundaneness are not meant to be separated. The mundane is meant to be tied to the holy and the holy is meant to have a presence in the mundane.

» Ordinary Jews are pivotal to bridging the holy and the mundane, for they live in the mundane world but are connected with G-d. Thus, G-d loves the ordinary Jew just as much, if not more, than He loves the holy Jew.

11.

Chukat—Balak

Trauma, Trauma, Wherefore Art Thou?

Reframing the Past to Fortify the Future

Dedicated in loving memory of
Rabbi Eliezer Elimelech Mangel,
הרה"ת השליח ר' אליעזר אלימלך בן יבלחט"א הרה"ח הר"ר ניסן שליט"א,
marking his yahrtzeit *on 4 Tamuz.*

And in appreciation to his siblings, יבלחט"א*, our partners who are sources of much valuable assistance and commitment to JLI's growth and success: Rabbi Yisroel Mangel (Cincinnati, OH), Rabbi Nochum Mangel (Dayton, OH), and Rabbi Mendel Mangel, (Cherry Hill, NJ)*

PARSHAH OVERVIEWS

Chukat

Moses is taught the laws of the red heifer, whose ashes purify a person who has been contaminated by contact with a dead body.

After forty years of journeying through the desert, the people of Israel arrive in the wilderness of Zin. Miriam dies, and the people thirst for water. G-d tells Moses to speak to a rock and command it to give water. Moses gets angry at the rebellious Israelites and strikes the stone. Water issues forth, but Moses is told by G-d that neither he nor Aaron will enter the Promised Land.

Aaron dies at Hor Hahar (Mount Hor) and is succeeded in the high priesthood by his son Eleazar. Venomous snakes attack the Israelite camp after yet another eruption of discontent in which the people "speak against G-d and Moses"; G-d tells Moses to place a brass serpent upon a high pole, and all who will gaze Heavenward will be healed. The people sing a song in honor of the miraculous well that provided them with water in the desert.

Moses leads the people in battles against the Emorite kings Sichon and Og (who seek to prevent Israel's passage through their territory) and conquers their lands, which lie east of the Jordan River.

Balak

Balak, the king of Mo'ab, summons the prophet Balaam to curse the people of Israel. On the way, Balaam is berated by his donkey, who sees, before Balaam does, the angel that G-d sends to block their way. Three times, from three different vantage points, Balaam attempts to pronounce his curses; each time, blessings issue forth instead. Balaam also prophesies on the end of days and the coming of Mashiach.

The people fall prey to the charms of the daughters of Mo'ab and are enticed to worship the idol Pe'or. When a high-ranking Israelite official publicly takes a Midianite princess into a tent, Phineas kills them both, stopping the plague raging among the people.

I. WHAT'S IN A NAME?

When It's Best to Let Go

TEXT 1

THE REBBE, RABBI MENACHEM MENDEL SCHNEERSON, *IGROT KODESH* 4, P. 130

ובנוגע לרפואתו, הנה:

1. בטח ממלא אחרי הוראת הרופאים.
2. יסיח דעתו כפי האפשרי מהתעמקות בענין בריאותו.
3. יהיה בטחונו חזק בה' יתברך, אשר אין מעצור לפניו ומי יאמר לו מה תעשה.
4. יתקשר בתוספות התקשרות לאילנא דחיי - היא תורת החסידות, דברי אלקים חיים.

With respect to your healing, I make the following recommendations:

1. Surely, you're following the instructions of your physicians.
2. To the extent that you can, stop dwelling on your health issues.
3. Strengthen your faith in G-d, for Whom nothing is impossible.
4. Strengthen your bond to the tree of life—the Torah of *Chasidut*, the living words of G-d.

Rabbi Menachem Mendel Schneerson 1902–1994

The towering Jewish leader of the 20th century, known as "the Lubavitcher Rebbe," or simply as "the Rebbe." Born in southern Ukraine, the Rebbe escaped Nazi-occupied Europe, arriving in the U.S. in June 1941. The Rebbe inspired and guided the revival of traditional Judaism after the European devastation, impacting virtually every Jewish community the world over. The Rebbe often emphasized that the performance of just one additional good deed could usher in the era of Mashiach. The Rebbe's scholarly talks and writings have been printed in more than 200 volumes.

The Greatest Antisemite in History

TEXT 2

MIDRASH, *TANCHUMA*, BALAK 2

וְשׂוֹנְאָן הָיָה יוֹתֵר מִכָּל שׂוֹנְאִים. שֶׁכֻּלָּם הָיוּ בָּאִין בְּמִלְחָמוֹת וּבְשִׁעְבּוּד שֶׁהֵן יְכוֹלִים לַעֲמֹד בָּהֶן. וְזֶה, כְּאָדָם שֶׁהוּא מוֹצִיא דָבָר מִפִּיו לַעֲקֹר אֻמָּה שְׁלֵמָה.

In the history of antisemites, there was no greater antisemite than Balak. All other antisemites attacked the Jews by war and bondage—something we could survive. Balak intended to weaponize [Balaam's] curses to destroy the entire nation.

Tanchuma

A Midrashic work bearing the name of Rabbi Tanchuma, a 4th-century Talmudic sage quoted often in this work. "Midrash" is the designation of a particular genre of rabbinic literature usually forming a running commentary on specific books of the Bible. *Tanchuma* provides textual exegeses, expounds upon the biblical narrative, and develops and illustrates moral principles. *Tanchuma* is unique in that many of its sections commence with a Halachic discussion, which subsequently leads into non-Halachic teachings.

Obliterate the Name

TEXT 3A

PROVERBS 10:7

וְשֵׁם רְשָׁעִים יִרְקָב.

The name of the wicked must be left to rot.

Proverbs

Biblical book. The book of Proverbs appears in the "Writings" section of the Bible and contains the wise teachings, aphorisms, and parables of King Solomon, who lived in the 9th century BCE. The ethical teachings of Proverbs give counsel about overcoming temptation, extol the value of hard work, laud the pursuit of knowledge, and emphasize loyalty to G-d and His commandments as the foundation of true wisdom.

TEXT 3B

MIDRASH, *BERESHIT RABAH* 49:1

אָמַר רַבִּי יִצְחָק: כָּל . . . מִי שֶׁהוּא מַזְכִּיר אֶת הָרָשָׁע וְאֵינוֹ מְקַלְּלוֹ, עוֹבֵר בַּעֲשֵׂה.

מַה טַעְמֵיהּ?

"וְשֵׁם רְשָׁעִים יִרְקָב" (מִשְׁלֵי י, ז).

Rabbi Yitzchak said, "One . . . who utters the name of a wicked person, but fails to add a curse, transgresses a positive commandment."

What is the source of this commandment?

"The name of the wicked must be left to rot" (Proverbs 10:7).

Bereshit Rabah

An early rabbinic commentary on the Book of Genesis. This Midrash bears the name of Rabbi Oshiya Rabah (Rabbi Oshiya "the Great"), whose teaching opens this work. This Midrash provides textual exegeses and stories, expounds upon the biblical narrative, and develops and illustrates moral principles. Produced by the sages of the Talmud in the Land of Israel, its use of Aramaic closely resembles that of the Jerusalem Talmud. It was first printed in Constantinople in 1512 together with 4 other Midrashic works on the other 4 books of the Pentateuch.

TEXT 3C

TALMUD, YOMA 38B

מַאי "וְשֵׁם רְשָׁעִים יִרְקָב" (מִשְׁלֵי י, ז)?

אָמַר רַבִּי אֶלְעָזָר: רַקְבִּיבוּת תַּעֲלֶה בִּשְׁמוֹתָן, דְּלָא מַסְקִינַן בִּשְׁמַיְיהוּ.

What is the meaning of, "The name of the wicked must be left to rot?"

Rabbi Elazar said, "Decay will spread on their names, for we will not name others by their names."

Babylonian Talmud

A literary work of monumental proportions that draws upon the legal, spiritual, intellectual, ethical, and historical traditions of Judaism. The 37 tractates of the Babylonian Talmud contain the teachings of the Jewish sages from the period after the destruction of the 2nd Temple through the 5th century CE. It has served as the primary vehicle for the transmission of the Oral Law and the education of Jews over the centuries; it is the entry point for all subsequent legal, ethical, and theological Jewish scholarship.

II. A PAGAN MENTION

The Parallel Law

TEXT 4A

EXODUS 23:13

ושם אלוקים אחרים לא תזכירו.

Do not mention the names of other gods.

TEXT 4B

TALMUD, SANHEDRIN 63B

"ושם אלקים אחרים לא תזכירו" (שמות כג, יג). שלא יאמר אדם לחבירו: שמור לי בצד עבודת כוכבים פלונית.

"Do not mention the names of other gods." For example, a person shouldn't say to someone else, "Wait for me beside a certain idol."

TEXT 4C

TALMUD, IBID.

כי אתא עולא, בת בקלנבו.

אמר ליה רבא: והיכא בת מר?

אמר ליה: בקלנבו.

אמר ליה: והכתיב "ושם אלקים אחרים לא תזכירו?"

אמר ליה: הכי אמר רבי יוחנן: כל עבודת כוכבים הכתובה בתורה, מותר להזכיר שמה.

When the sage Ula arrived, he overnighted in Kalenbo [a city named after the idol around which it was built].

Rava asked him, "Where did the master overnight?"

Ula replied, "In Kalenbo."

Rava said, "But does the passage not state, 'Do not mention the names of other gods?'"

Ula replied, "So taught Rabbi Yochanan, 'We are permitted to mention the name of any idol that appears in the Torah.'"

G-d, Not Us

TEXT 5A

DAAT ZEKENIM BAALEI HATOSAFOT, EXODUS 14:2

"לפני בעל צפון" . . . תמה להרב רבי יהודה, היאך אמר לו שיחנו על הים לפני בעל צפון, והא אמרינן: אסור לאדם לומר לחבירו המתן לי בצד עבודב זרה פלונית?

צריך עיון.

ולי נראה, דדוקא לאדם. אבל להקדוש ברוך הוא לא.

"In front of *baal tzefon*." . . . [I saw that] Rabbi Yehudah wondered why G-d instructed Moses to have the Jews settle near the ocean in front of *baal tzefon*. Do we not say that it is forbidden to tell our fellow, "Wait for me before a certain idol"?

[Rabbi Yehudah concluded by observing that] this is a difficult matter that requires deeper analysis.

It seems to me that the answer is simple. This prohibition was only ever binding on humankind. It was never binding on G-d.

Tosafot

A collection of French and German Talmudic commentaries written during the 12th and 13th centuries. Among the most famous authors of *Tosafot* are Rabbi Yaakov Tam, Rabbi Shimshon ben Avraham of Sens, and Rabbi Yitzchak ("the Ri"). Printed in almost all editions of the Talmud, these commentaries are fundamental to basic Talmudic study.

Obliteration

TEXT 5B

RABBI ELIEZER OF METZ, *SEFER YERE'IM*, CH. 245

כל עבודת כוכבים הכתובה בתורה מותר להזכיר.

וטעמא: כיון שהזכיה, ודאי נתבטלה.

Any idol mentioned in the Torah may be mentioned.

The reason: once it is mentioned in the Torah, it has certainly been obliterated.

Rabbi Eliezer of Metz
c. 1140–c. 1125

Talmudic scholar and Halachic authority. Rabbi Eliezer of Metz, France, was a student of Rabbi Yaakov Tam, the leader of the Tosafist school of Talmudic scholarship. He is known for *Sefer Yere'im*, a work that incorporates Halachah and ethics in its examination of all of the 613 commandments.

Difficulties with the Explanations

TEXT 6

MIDRASH, *SHEMOT RABAH* 30:9

שֶׁאֵין מִדּוֹתָיו שֶׁל הַקָּדוֹשׁ בָּרוּךְ הוּא כְּמִדַּת בָּשָׂר וָדָם.
מִדַּת בָּשָׂר וָדָם מוֹרֶה לַאֲחֵרִים לַעֲשׂוֹת וְהוּא אֵינוֹ עוֹשֶׂה כְּלוּם. וְהַקָּדוֹשׁ בָּרוּךְ הוּא אֵינוֹ כֵן, אֶלָּא מַה שֶּׁהוּא עוֹשֶׂה, הוּא אוֹמֵר לְיִשְׂרָאֵל לַעֲשׂוֹת.

G-d is different from human lords.

A human lord tells others what to do and does nothing himself. G-d is different. What He does, He tells the Jewish people to do.

Shemot Rabah

An early rabbinic commentary on the Book of Exodus. "Midrash" is the designation of a particular genre of rabbinic literature usually forming a running commentary on specific books of the Bible. *Shemot Rabah*, written mostly in Hebrew, provides textual exegeses, expounds upon the biblical narrative, and develops and illustrates moral principles. It was first printed in Constantinople in 1512 together with 4 other Midrashic works on the other 4 books of the Pentateuch.

Effective Obliteration

TEXT 7

THE REBBE, RABBI MENACHEM MENDEL SCHNEERSON,
LIKUTEI SICHOT 23, PP. 168-169

ויש לומה, אז דער פשט אין יראים איז, אז די עבודה זרה "ודאי נתבטלה" ביי דעם איד . . . וואס דערמאנט איר:

כשם ווי דאס וואס תורה דערמאנט עניני (ושמות) עבודה זרה, איז דאך דאס אויף צו ארויסברענגען אז זיי זיינען אפס והבל ואין בם מועיל וממש, זייער פאלשקייט, און דער טעות פון די וואס האבן געדינט די עבודה זרה . . .

קומט אויס, אז די הזכרת שם עבודה זרה בתורה ברענגט היפך וביטול החשיבות פון דער עבודה זרה, אדרבה - דאס איז מדגיש דעם שקר של העבודה זרה.

איז על דרך זה ביי א אידן: ווען ער דערמאנט א שם עבודה זרה הכתוב בתורה - איז דאס בהתוכן ווי ער איז כתוב בתורה - היפך החשיבות וממשות פון דער עבודה זרה, אזא עבודה זרה (וואס תורה האט שוין קלאר ארויסגעבראכט אז אין בה ממש) איז ביי אים "ודאי נתבטלה", ובמילא (ווי דער יראים איז ממשיך) - "מאותה טעם שהתורה מזכרת אותה (- אויף ארויסצוברענגען אז זי איז אפס) אנו רשאין להזכירה".

To answer: Rabbi Eliezer ben Shimon meant to say that [names of false deities mentioned in the Torah] are obliterated in the minds of Jews who mention them.

When the Torah mentions the name of a false deity, it is certainly to underscore its vanity, emptiness, and absolute lack of power. The Torah seeks to highlight the idol's utter falsehood and the error of those who worshipped it.

It follows that the appearance of a false deity's name in the Torah reverses and nullifies any supposition that it might have power. On the contrary, it underlines the idol's emptiness and falsehood.

By the same token, when we mention the names of idols that appear in the Torah with similar intention, we too dismiss the idol's importance and substance. Idols that the Torah revealed to be without substance are as good as obliterated in our minds when we mention their names.

Under such conditions, we are permitted to mention the name of the idol for the same reason that the Torah mentions it.

Defending the First Explanation

TEXT 8

THE REBBE, RABBI MENACHEM MENDEL SCHNEERSON, *LIKUTEI SICHOT* 23, P. 169

> ווען אן אדם דערמאנט א שם עבודה זרה איז דאך רצונו להזכירה (ובפרט ווען דאס איז א הזכרה לצורך) איז ער דערמיט מחשיב די עבודה זרה. אבער מצד הקדוש ברוך הוא, איז ניטא קיין ארט חס ושלום פאר דעם טעות פון עבודה זרה.
>
> ואדרבה, דער "תוכן" פון דעם וואס דער אויבערשטער אלקים אמת זאגט דעם שם עבודה זרה (אדער עס שטייט אין תורת אמת), דערמיט גופא ווערט די עבודה זרה נתבטל, דיבור וגילוי האמת - איז מבטל ושולל אפילו א קא סלקא דעתך פון דעם שקר פון דער עבודה זרה...
>
> און על דרך זה איז עס ביי א אידן: ווען ער דערמאנט א שם עבודה זרה (הכתובה בתורה) אין דעם אופן ווי זי איז כתובה בתורה - איז ער דערמיט מזכיר ומדגיש דעם ביטול פון דער עבודה זרה.

When ordinary people mention the name of an idol, their intention is to use it as a reference, especially if they mention it for a significant purpose [such as referencing a meeting place. Unintentional as it might be,] using the idol as a reference lends it significance. From G-d's perspective, however, the error of attributing significance to idolatry is impossible.

On the contrary, when the true G-d mentions a false deity's name (or if it appears in His Torah), it is, perforce, nullified. The very articulation and revelation of absolute truth dismisses and excludes even the glimmer of a supposition that an idol is anything but utter falsehood.

Similarly, when ordinary Jews, in this same spirit, utter an idol's name that appears in the Torah, they too they too highlight and underline the idol's complete lack of power.

III. SHRIVEL IN THE GLARE OF LIGHT

The Parallel

TEXT 9

RABBI CHAIM YOSEF DAVID AZULAI, *YOSEF OMETZ*, 11

אמרו בסנהדרין (סג, ב), אמר רבי יוחנן: כל עבודת כוכבים הכתובה בתורה, מותר להזכיר שמה.

וכי היכי דהתורה הזכירה שמות הרשעים, יהא שרי לן להזכירן.

Rabbi Yochanan taught, "We are permitted to mention the name of any idol that appears in the Torah" (Sanhedrin 63b).

Similarly, we should be permitted to mention names of wicked people that appear in the Torah.

Rabbi Chaim Yosef David Azulai (Chida)
1724–1806

Talmudist and noted bibliophile. Born in Jerusalem, scion to a prominent rabbinic family, he studied under Rabbi Chaim ibn Atar. A prolific writer on various Jewish topics, his *Shem Hagedolim* is particularly famous, chronicling short biographies of Jewish authors with overviews of their works. He traveled extensively in Europe to raise funds on behalf of the Jewish community in the Land of Israel, and died in Italy.

Returning to Balak

TEXT 10

THE REBBE, RABBI MENACHEM MENDEL SCHNEERSON, *LIKUTEI SICHOT* 23, P. 170

כשם ווי דאס וואס תורה דערציילט וועגן בלק, איז דאס כדי צו ארויסברענגען ווי עס איז צעשטערט געווארן מחשבתו הרעה "לכה נא ארה לי את העם הזה גו' אולי אוכל נכה בו גו'" (במדבר כב, ו), און דערפאר איז דאס ניט קיין סתירה צו "שם רשעים ירקב" (משלי י, ז), ווייל אדרבה - אזא דערמאנונג איז נאך מוסיף אין דעם גנאי ורקב פון דעם שם הרשע.

על דרך זה אויך בנוגע דער קריאת שם הסדרה מיטן נאמען בלק: ווען אידן נוצן דעם שם "בלק" אלס דעם נאמען פון א סדרה בתורה, מיינען זיי דאך "בלק" ווי תורה רעדט וועגן אים, וואס דאס איז א זכרון (ניט לשם זכרון, נאר פארקערט) וואס קומט ארויסברענגען דעם גנאי פון בלק.

The Torah tells the story of Balak to broadcast the breakdown of his evil plan. He said to Balaam, "Please come and curse these people for me; . . . perhaps I will be able to wage war against them" (Numbers 22:6) [and this plan was foiled]. This is not in conflict with the dictum, "The name of the wicked must be left to rot" (Proverbs 10:7). On the contrary, such mention increases his shame and accelerates the rot of his wicked name.

The same is true of naming the Torah portion after Balak. When we use the name Balak in reference to a Torah portion, we refer to him as the Torah does—not to perpetuate his name, but to amplify his shame.

We Were Lifted Up

TEXT 11

THE REBBE, RABBI MENACHEM MENDEL SCHNEERSON, IBID., PP. 170–171

ביי בלק געפינט מען, אז ניט נאר איז מחשבתו הרעה צעשטערט געווארן (על דרך דעם ענין פון ביטול עבודה זרה), נאר נאכמער: זיין דינגען בלעם'ן האט געבראכט א הוספה צו אידן - אז אידן זאלן געבענטשט ווערן מיט ברכות נעלות ביותר - וואס דאס איז א גרעסערער אויפטו פון דעם וואס ווערט אויפגעטאן דורך ביטול עבודה זרה:

בשעת מ'איז מבטל עבודה זרה, וואס די עבודה זרה עצמה איז דאך א "כפירה באחדותו" מוז זי אינגאנצן נתבטל ווערן. מה שאין כן מעשה בלק, האט זיין רשעות, זיין שנאה צו אידן וואס דערפאר האט ער געדונגען בלעם'ן, אויף "לכה נא ארה לי גו'", געבראכט א סיוע והוספה צו אידן (ברכות נעלות ביותר).

און דאס איז אויך וואס מ'רופט אן די סדרה "בלק", ווייל דורך אים (און זיין דינגען בלעם) איז ארויסגעקומען א יתרון ביי אידן.

Balak's evil intentions were not only neutralized—as when an idol is obliterated. Rather, hiring Balaam also helped the Jews. It resulted in transcendental blessings for the Jewish people. This is a much greater achievement than neutralizing a false deity.

When we nullify a false deity—a denial of G-d's unity—we must obliterate it. Balak's story is different. The wickedness and hatred that caused him to hire Balaam to curse the Jews [were not merely neutralized. They] ended up aiding the Jews with transcendental blessings.

This is an even deeper reason for naming the Torah portion after Balak. Through him, more accurately by him hiring Balaam, the destiny of the Jewish people was enhanced.

Why We Tell the Story

TEXT 12A

PROVERBS 3:25

אַל תִּירָא מִפַּחַד פִּתְאֹם וּמִשֹּׁאַת רְשָׁעִים כִּי תָבֹא.

Fear not sudden terror or the destruction of the wicked when it comes.

TEXT 12B

ISAIAH 8:10

עֻצוּ עֵצָה וְתֻפָר, דַּבְּרוּ דָבָר וְלֹא יָקוּם, כִּי עִמָּנוּ קֵל.

They may take counsel, but it will be foiled. They may speak words, but [their plan] will not succeed, for G-d is with us.

Isaiah

Biblical book. The Book of Isaiah contains the prophecies of Isaiah, who lived in the 7th–6th centuries BCE. Isaiah's prophecies contain stern rebukes for the personal failings of the contemporary people of Judea and the corruption of its government. The bulk of the prophecies, however, are stirring consolations and poetic visions of the future Redemption.

Conclusion

TEXT 13A

THE REBBE, RABBI MENACHEM MENDEL SCHNEERSON, *IGROT KODESH* 25, P. 57

מ'זעט דאך באשיינפערלעך, אז דער זכרון פון אומעטיקע זאכן בכלל, און פון אזוינע מאוים'דיקע פאסירונגען בפרט - איז צום אלעם ערשטן פארשטארקט דאס דעם פעסימיזם.

און במילא שוואכט עס אפ אויך די ענערגיע, וואס דאס ווירקט זיך אויס אין א היפך פון בויען און שאפן, צו וועלכע עס פאדערט זיך דוקא בטחון און שמחה.

We can plainly see that sad memories, especially horrific memories, enhance our pessimism [for the present and future].

In turn, pessimism depletes our energy, which shuts down all creativity and efforts to rebuild. For such enterprises specifically require trust in G-d and a joyful disposition.

TEXT 13B

THE REBBE, RABBI MENACHEM MENDEL SCHNEERSON, IBID., PP. 56–57

אין אונזער תקופה, ווי טייער עס זאל זיין דער זכרון פון אונזערע קדושים, השם ינקום דמם, און ווי נויטווענדיק עס איז אז אונזער דור זאל וויסן וועגן דער שואה, על אחת כמה וכמה ניט פארגעסן די ענינים פון קידוש השם וואס מ'האט געזען פון די קדושים . . .

איז אבער פון דער אנדער זייט נאך וויכטיקער צו געדענקען די איבערוויגענדע פליכט - באזירנדיק זיך אויף אונזערע חכמי המשנה, אז מעשה הוא העיקר - צו טאן דעם מאקסימום אום צו בויען דאס לעבן פון אידן און דעם אידישן לעבן, אין כמות און אין איכות, אין דער פולסטער מאס.

און דאס איז אויך דער ריכטיקער ענטפער און די ריכטיקע מלחמה מיט היטלערן און זיינע יורשים, וואס ליידער ווערן זיי ניט ווייניקער און אפשר גאר פארקערט, כאטש זיי דערשיינען אונטער פארשידענע צורות און מאסקעראדן.

In our post-Holocaust era, we cherish the memory of the sacred martyrs, may G-d avenge their deaths. It is important that our generation know about the Shoah, and even more important that they never forget that the six million sanctified G-d's name. . . .

On the other hand, considering the teaching of our sages that action is primary, it is most important that we remember our greatest obligation: to respond to the Holocaust by doing all that we can to rebuild the lives of Jews and the verve of Jewish life in the greatest quantitative and qualitative measures. . . .

This the correct response and the correct war to wage against Hitler and his successors, may their names be obliterated, who sadly, rather than having decreased, have perhaps even increased, albeit in alternate forms and guises.

APPENDIX

TEXT 14A

MISHNAH, AVODAH ZARAH 3:4

שָׁאַל פְּרוֹקְלוֹס בֶּן פְּלוֹסְפוֹס אֶת רַבָּן גַּמְלִיאֵל בְּעַכּוֹ, שֶׁהָיָה רוֹחֵץ בַּמֶּרְחָץ שֶׁל אַפְרוֹדִיטִי. אָמַר לוֹ: כָּתוּב בְּתוֹרַתְכֶם "וְלֹא יִדְבַּק בְּיָדְךָ מְאוּמָה מִן הַחֵרֶם" (דְּבָרִים יג, יח), מִפְּנֵי מָה אַתָּה רוֹחֵץ בַּמֶּרְחָץ שֶׁל אַפְרוֹדִיטִי?

אָמַר לוֹ: אֵין מְשִׁיבִין בַּמֶּרְחָץ.

וּכְשֶׁיָּצָא אָמַר לוֹ: אֲנִי לֹא בָאתִי בִגְבוּלָהּ, הִיא בָאתָה בִגְבוּלִי.

While bathing in the city of Akko in the bathhouse of the Greek goddess Aphrodite, Proclus son of Plospus asked the following of Rabban Gamliel: "Your Torah states, 'No forbidden item [hitherto used for idol worship] may cleave to your hand' (Deuteronomy 13:18). Why do you bathe in the bathhouse of Aphrodite?"

Rabban Gamliel replied, "One may not answer questions related to Torah in the bathhouse."

When he left the bathhouse, Rabban Gamliel said, "I did not come into its domain; it entered my domain."

Mishnah

The first authoritative work of Jewish law that was codified in writing. The Mishnah contains the oral traditions that were passed down from teacher to student; it supplements, clarifies, and systematizes the commandments of the Torah. Due to the continual persecution of the Jewish people, it became increasingly difficult to guarantee that these traditions would not be forgotten. Rabbi Yehudah Hanasi therefore redacted the Mishnah at the end of the 2nd century. It serves as the foundation for the Talmud.

TEXT 14B

RABBI YA'IR CHAIM BACHARACH, *CHAVOT YA'IR* 1:11–12

דגוים בזמן הזה לאו עובדי עבודה זרה נינהו לכל מילי, אחר מאמינים בורא שמים וארץ יתברך שמו.

Non-Jews today are not idol worshippers since they believe in the Creator of Heaven and earth, may His name be blessed.

Rabbi Ya'ir Chaim Bacharach
1638–1702

Halachic authority. Rabbi Ya'ir Chaim Bacharach was raised in Worms, Germany, where his father, Rabbi Moshe Shimon, was a rabbi and preacher. Rabbi Ya'ir Chaim served as a rabbi in the communities of Mainz, Koblenz, and Worms, all in Germany. He wrote a number of Halachic works, including *Mekor Chaim*, a commentary on the Code of Jewish Law, and is best known for his work of responsa, *Chavot Ya'ir*. His writings show his independence as a Halachic authority, as well as his broad knowledge in the fields of astronomy, mathematics, and philosophy.

TEXT 14C

RABBI YA'IR CHAIM BACHARACH, IBID.

כי המון עם מחזיקים לעון וחירוף הזכרת שם הנעבד כמו שקורין עובדיו, וכן שם אמו. וראוי להניחם על מנהגם.

The average Jew [has always] considered it sinful and blasphemous to mention the name that is used by those who worship him. This custom should remain unchanged. This applies equally to the name of this man's mother.

KEY POINTS

- The names of the wicked may only be mentioned if accompanied by a curse such as, "May his name be obliterated."
- The name of an idol may only be mentioned if it appears in the Torah. Its appearance in the Torah, perforce, reveals its utter lack of substance. Thus, we can also say it with total revulsion and ridicule.
- We don't dwell on the names of wicked people and the terrible things they did. Similarly, we don't dwell on the memory of trauma and let it define us. We focus on living our lives.
- However, if the memory of the trauma can be channeled and framed in a positive, life-affirming way, it behooves us to remember it and to frame it that way.
- This is especially true for traumas that are too large to forget, and any attempt to do so would backfire.

12.

Pinchas

Why You Must Learn from Your Own Mistakes

Some Things Cannot Be Taught. They Must Be Learned and Earned.

Dedicated in loving memory of Dr. Gary Toback,
אפרים גרשום בן ישראל ע"ה,
marking his yahrtzeit *on 14 Tamuz.*

May the merit of the Torah study worldwide accompany his soul in the world of everlasting life and be a source of blessings to his family, with much health, happiness, nachas, *and success.*

PARSHAH OVERVIEW

Pinchas

Aaron's grandson Phineas is rewarded for his act of zealotry in killing the Simeonite prince Zimri and the Midianite princess who was his paramour: G-d grants him a covenant of peace and the priesthood.

A census of the people counts 601,730 men between the ages of twenty and sixty. Moses is instructed on how the Land is to be divided by lottery among the tribes and families of Israel. The five daughters of Zelophehad petition Moses that they be granted the portion of the Land belonging to their father, who died without sons; G-d accepts their claim and incorporates it into the Torah's laws of inheritance.

Moses empowers Joshua to succeed him and lead the people into the Land of Israel.

The *parshah* concludes with a detailed list of the daily offerings and the additional offerings brought on Shabbat; Rosh Chodesh (the first day of the month); and the festivals of Passover, Shavuot, and Sukkot.

INTRODUCTION

Exercise

What other types of life skills and truths can only be learned?

What kinds of life lessons can we only learn from our own mistakes, even if others made the mistakes before us and tried to teach us?

Question for Discussion

Is there anything like that in Judaism?

Is there any part of Judaism that we can't learn from our parents and teachers and must come to on our own?

I. TWO UNKNOWN LAWS

Our Father's Land

TEXT 1A

NUMBERS 27:1–5

א. וַתִּקְרַבְנָה בְּנוֹת צְלָפְחָד בֶּן חֵפֶר בֶּן גִּלְעָד בֶּן מָכִיר בֶּן מְנַשֶּׁה לְמִשְׁפְּחֹת
מְנַשֶּׁה בֶן יוֹסֵף, וְאֵלֶּה שְׁמוֹת בְּנֹתָיו, מַחְלָה נֹעָה וְחָגְלָה וּמִלְכָּה וְתִרְצָה.

ב. וַתַּעֲמֹדְנָה לִפְנֵי מֹשֶׁה וְלִפְנֵי אֶלְעָזָר הַכֹּהֵן וְלִפְנֵי הַנְּשִׂיאִם וְכָל הָעֵדָה,
פֶּתַח אֹהֶל מוֹעֵד, לֵאמֹר.

ג. אָבִינוּ מֵת בַּמִּדְבָּר וְהוּא לֹא הָיָה בְּתוֹךְ הָעֵדָה הַנּוֹעָדִים עַל ה' בַּעֲדַת
קֹרַח, כִּי בְחֶטְאוֹ מֵת וּבָנִים לֹא הָיוּ לוֹ.

ד. לָמָּה יִגָּרַע שֵׁם אָבִינוּ מִתּוֹךְ מִשְׁפַּחְתּוֹ כִּי אֵין לוֹ בֵּן, תְּנָה לָּנוּ אֲחֻזָּה בְּתוֹךְ
אֲחֵי אָבִינוּ.

ה. וַיַּקְרֵב מֹשֶׁה אֶת מִשְׁפָּטָן לִפְנֵי ה'.

1. The daughters of Zelophehad, of the Manassite family—son of Hepher, son of Gilead, son of Machir, son of Manasseh, son of Joseph—came forward. The names of the daughters were Mahlah, Noah, Hoglah, Milcah, and Tirzah.

2. They stood before Moses, Eleazar the priest, the chieftains, and the whole assembly, at the entrance of the Tent of Meeting, and they said:

3. "Our father died in the wilderness. He did not belong to Korah's faction, which banded together against G-d, rather he died for his own sin, and he has left no sons.

4. "Let not our father's name be lost to his clan just because he had no son. Give us a holding among our father's kinsmen."

5. Moses brought their case before G-d.

TEXT 1B

IBID., 25:6-8

ו. וַיֹּאמֶר ה' אֶל מֹשֶׁה לֵּאמֹר.

ז. כֵּן בְּנוֹת צְלָפְחָד דֹּבְרֹת, נָתֹן תִּתֵּן לָהֶם אֲחֻזַּת נַחֲלָה בְּתוֹךְ אֲחֵי אֲבִיהֶם, וְהַעֲבַרְתָּ אֶת נַחֲלַת אֲבִיהֶן לָהֶן.

ח. וְאֶל בְּנֵי יִשְׂרָאֵל תְּדַבֵּר לֵאמֹר, אִישׁ כִּי יָמוּת וּבֵן אֵין לוֹ וְהַעֲבַרְתֶּם אֶת נַחֲלָתוֹ לְבִתּוֹ.

6. G-d spoke to Moses saying:

7. "Zelophehad's daughters speak justly. Certainly, give them a portion of inheritance along with their father's brothers, and transfer their father's inheritance to them.

8. "Speak to the Children of Israel saying, 'If a man dies and has no son, transfer his inheritance to his daughter.'"

The Second Passover

TEXT 2A

NUMBERS 9:6–11

ו. וַיְהִי אֲנָשִׁים אֲשֶׁר הָיוּ טְמֵאִים לְנֶפֶשׁ אָדָם וְלֹא יָכְלוּ לַעֲשֹׂת הַפֶּסַח
בַּיּוֹם הַהוּא, וַיִּקְרְבוּ לִפְנֵי מֹשֶׁה וְלִפְנֵי אַהֲרֹן בַּיּוֹם הַהוּא.

ז. וַיֹּאמְרוּ הָאֲנָשִׁים הָהֵמָּה אֵלָיו, אֲנַחְנוּ טְמֵאִים לְנֶפֶשׁ אָדָם, לָמָּה נִגָּרַע
לְבִלְתִּי הַקְרִב אֶת קָרְבַּן ה' בְּמֹעֲדוֹ בְּתוֹךְ בְּנֵי יִשְׂרָאֵל.

ח. וַיֹּאמֶר אֲלֵהֶם מֹשֶׁה, עִמְדוּ וְאֶשְׁמְעָה מַה יְצַוֶּה ה' לָכֶם.

ט. וַיְדַבֵּר ה' אֶל מֹשֶׁה לֵּאמֹר.

י. דַּבֵּר אֶל בְּנֵי יִשְׂרָאֵל לֵאמֹר, אִישׁ אִישׁ כִּי יִהְיֶה טָמֵא לָנֶפֶשׁ אוֹ בְדֶרֶךְ
רְחֹקָה לָכֶם אוֹ לְדֹרֹתֵיכֶם, וְעָשָׂה פֶסַח לַה'.

יא. בַּחֹדֶשׁ הַשֵּׁנִי בְּאַרְבָּעָה עָשָׂר יוֹם בֵּין הָעַרְבַּיִם יַעֲשׂוּ אֹתוֹ, עַל מַצּוֹת
וּמְרֹרִים יֹאכְלֻהוּ.

6. There were men who were ritually impure [because of contact with] a dead person, and therefore could not offer the Passover sacrifice on that day. They approached Moses and Aaron on that day.

7. Those men said to him, "We are ritually unclean [because of contact] with a dead person; why should we be excluded so as not to bring the offering of the L-rd in its appointed time, with all the Children of Israel?"

8. Moses said to them, "Wait, and I will hear what G-d will instruct you to do."

9. G-d spoke to Moses, saying:

10. "Speak to the Children of Israel saying: Any person who becomes unclean from [contact with] the dead, or is on a distant journey, whether among you or in future generations, should offer a Passover sacrifice to G-d.

11. "They should offer it in the second month, on the fourteenth day, in the afternoon; they should eat it with matzot and bitter herbs."

The Study Hall

TEXT 2B

RASHI, NUMBERS 9:6

"לפני משה ולפני אהרן". כששניהם יושבין בבית המדרש באו ושאלום. ולא יתכן לומר זה אחר זה, שאם משה לא היה יודע, אהרן מנין לו?

"Before Moses and Aaron." They asked both, as both were seated in the study hall. One cannot suggest that they asked Aaron after Moses because if Moses didn't know, how would Aaron know?

Rabbi Shlomo Yitzchaki (Rashi)
1040–1105

Most noted biblical and Talmudic commentator. Born in Troyes, France, Rashi studied in the famed *yeshivot* of Mainz and Worms. His commentaries on the Pentateuch and the Talmud, which focus on the straightforward meaning of the text, appear in virtually every edition of the Talmud and Bible.

TEXT 2C

RASHI, NUMBERS 27:2

"לפני משה". ואחר כך לפני אלעזר. אפשר אם משה לא ידע אלעזר יודע? . . .

אבא חנן משום רבי אלעזר אומר: בבית המדרש היו יושבים, ועמדו לפני כולם.

"Before Moses" and then before Eleazar. If Moses didn't know, how would Eleazar know? . . .

Aba Chanan said in the name of Rabbi Eleazar, "They were all seated in the study hall, and the daughters stood [to speak] before [them] all at once."

II. THE FESTIVAL OF SELF-INSPIRATION

Not by Default

TEXT 3

THE REBBE, RABBI MENACHEM MENDEL SCHNEERSON, *LIKUTEI SICHOT* 18, P. 118

דער חילוק, אין פשטות, צווישן פסח ראשון און פסח שני איז:

פסח ראשון איז דער אופן החיוב פון הקרבת הפסח ווי ס'איז אויסגעשטעלט און דארף זיין על פי סדר פון תורה (בזמנו); פסח שני איז אופן החיוב שלא על פי סדר (שלא בזמנו):

די וואס האבן ניט געבראכט דעם פסח בזמנו – אף על פי כן זאגט מען ניט עבר יומו בטל קרבנו נאר תורה גיט די געלעגנהייט צו ברענגען דעם קרבן שפעטער.

What is the difference between the first and the second Passover?

The first Passover is the default method of discharging the paschal offering obligation—on the date assigned by the Torah. The second Passover is activated when one discharges one's obligation in a disorderly manner—on the incorrect date.

Those who failed to bring the paschal offering on time did not lose their chance. The Torah made an exception and offered them a second opportunity.

Rabbi Menachem Mendel Schneerson 1902–1994

The towering Jewish leader of the 20th century, known as "the Lubavitcher Rebbe," or simply as "the Rebbe." Born in southern Ukraine, the Rebbe escaped Nazi-occupied Europe, arriving in the U.S. in June 1941. The Rebbe inspired and guided the revival of traditional Judaism after the European devastation, impacting virtually every Jewish community the world over. The Rebbe often emphasized that the performance of just one additional good deed could usher in the era of Mashiach. The Rebbe's scholarly talks and writings have been printed in more than 200 volumes.

TEXT 4

THE REBBE, RABBI MENACHEM MENDEL SCHNEERSON, IBID., P. 119

ס'איז בדוגמא צום אונטערשייד צווישן דער עבודה פון א צדיק אדער פון א בעל תשובה:

א צדיק דינט דעם אויבערשטן לויטן דרך הישר – "אשר עשה האלקים את האדם ישר" – על פי סדר דתורה. א בעל תשובה וואס האט עובר געווען אויף סדר התורה, גיט אים דער אויבערשטער די מעגליכקייט צו פאריכטן דעם עבר און משלים זיין החסר.

The [difference between the two Passovers is like the] difference between a righteous person and a penitent.

The righteous person serves G-d in the way that the Torah establishes—he is upright. A penitent is one who has transgressed the Torah's proper order. Now G-d provides the opportunity to correct the past and fill in what was lacking.

TEXT 5

THE REBBE, RABBI MENACHEM MENDEL SCHNEERSON, *HAYOM YOM*, 14 IYAR

פסח שני ענינו איז – עס איז ניטא קיין "פארפאלען".

מען קען אלע מאל פאריכטען. אפילו מי שהיה טמא, מי שהיה בדרך רחוקה, און אפילו "לכם", אז דאס איז געווען ברצונו, פונדעסטוועגען קען מען מתקן זיין.

The theme of the second Passover is that it is never too late; we can always make things right.

Even if one was ritually impure or at a distance, and even in a case when it was deliberate, it can nonetheless be corrected.

Hayom Yom

In 1942, Rabbi Yosef Yitzchak Schneersohn, the 6th rebbe of Chabad, gave his son-in-law, the future Rebbe, the task of compiling an anthology of Chasidic aphorisms and customs arranged according to the days of the year. In describing the completed product, Rabbi Yosef Yitzchak wrote that it is "a book that is small in format but bursting with pearls and diamonds of the choicest quality."

When the Door Is Slammed

TEXT 6

THE REBBE, RABBI MENACHEM MENDEL SCHNEERSON, *LIKUTEI SICHOT* 18, P. 120

די תנועה פון תשובה קומט (בדרך כלל) דורך דער התעוררות פון דעם בעל תשובה: כאטש ער איז אין א מצב פון "טמא לנפש אדם" – היפך דטהרה ועל אחת כמה וכמה ניט קדושה, ער איז ניט שייך צו דערהערן א גילוי אור מלמעלה, דאך ווערט ער נתעורר מצד עצמו – מלמטה למעלה, בתשובה.

As a rule, the inspiration for repentance comes from within [not from G-d]. Penitents are in a spiritual state of impurity: "Their soul is impure" [Numbers 9:6]. In the present, their mindset is not one of purity, and they are certainly not in a holy mindset—they are uninspired by G-dliness. Nevertheless, they find their own way to repentance. Repentance is, by definition, self-inspired.

Greater Vigor

TEXT 7A

TALMUD, BERACHOT 34B

מָקוֹם שֶׁבַּעֲלֵי תְּשׁוּבָה עוֹמְדִין, אֵין צַדִּיקִים גְּמוּרִין יְכוֹלִין לַעֲמֹד בּוֹ.

The pedestal upon which penitents stand cannot be reached by those who are perfectly righteous.

Babylonian Talmud

A literary work of monumental proportions that draws upon the legal, spiritual, intellectual, ethical, and historical traditions of Judaism. The 37 tractates of the Babylonian Talmud contain the teachings of the Jewish sages from the period after the destruction of the 2nd Temple through the 5th century CE. It has served as the primary vehicle for the transmission of the Oral Law and the education of Jews over the centuries; it is the entry point for all subsequent legal, ethical, and theological Jewish scholarship.

TEXT 7B

ZOHAR, VOL. 1, P. 129B

רבי יוסי אמר: תנינן, אתר דמאריהון דתשובה קיימי ביה בההוא עלמא, צדיקים גמורים לית לון רשו לקיימא ביה, בגין דאינון קריבין למלכא יתיר מכולהו, ואינון משכי עלייהו ברעותא דלבא יתיה, ובחילא סגיא לאתקרבא למלכא.

Rabbi Yosei said, "We learned that perfectly righteous people have no permission to enter the Heavenly space occupied by those who repented on earth. This is because penitents are closer to G-d and are drawn to G-d with more passion than everyone else. They are drawn ever closer to G-d with intense vigor."

Zohar

The seminal work of kabbalah, Jewish mysticism. The *Zohar* is a mystical commentary on the Torah, written in Aramaic and Hebrew. According to the Arizal, the *Zohar* contains the teachings of Rabbi Shimon bar Yocha'i, who lived in the Land of Israel during the 2nd century. The *Zohar* has become one of the indispensable texts of traditional Judaism, alongside and nearly equal in stature to the Mishnah and Talmud.

Deeper Appreciation

TEXT 8

THE REBBE, RABBI MENACHEM MENDEL SCHNEERSON, LETTER, II ADAR 8, 5727 (MARCH 20, 1967), WWW.CHABAD.ORG/1898668

To be sure, that period of time in the past when the daily life should have been different requires rectification, especially by means of a determined effort to improve the present and future, so as to make up for the past.

On the other hand, human nature is such that things that come easily are taken for granted, and are not so appreciated and cherished as things for which one had to fight and struggle. Thus, the level of *Yiddishkeit* which you and your husband have attained through real efforts has permeated you more deeply and thoroughly.

May G-d grant that you should both continue in this direction together with your children, without allowing yourself to be hindered or influenced in any way by the difficulties which you describe in your letter.

On the contrary, the difficulties themselves can serve as a challenge and stimulus to greater spiritual advancement, as is also explained in Chassidic literature. . . .

III. DAUGHTERS OF ZELOPHEHAD

Moses Forgot

TEXT 9

RABBI SHNEUR ZALMAN OF LIADI, *TANYA, LIKUTEI AMARIM*, CH. 37

הַשִּׁכְחָה הִיא מִקְּלִיפַּת הַגּוּף וְנֶפֶשׁ הַחִיּוּנִית הַבַּהֲמִית.

Forgetfulness stems from G-d being concealed in the body and in the soul that vitalizes it.

Rabbi Shneur Zalman of Liadi (Alter Rebbe)
1745–1812

Chasidic rebbe, Halachic authority, and founder of the Chabad movement. The Alter Rebbe was born in Liozna, Belarus, and was among the principal students of the Magid of Mezeritch. His numerous works include the *Tanya*, an early classic containing the fundamentals of Chabad Chasidism; and *Shulchan Aruch HaRav*, an expanded and reworked code of Jewish law.

TEXT 10

RASHI, NUMBERS 27:5

נתעלמה הלכה ממנו.

וכאן נפרע על שנטל עטרה לומר "והדבר אשר יקשה מכם תקריבון אלי" (דברים א, יז).

The law eluded him.

Here, he was punished for crowning himself [with authority] by saying, "And any case that is too difficult for you, bring to me" (Deuteronomy 1:17).

The Study Hall

TEXT 11

THE REBBE, RABBI MENACHEM MENDEL SCHNEERSON,
LIKUTEI SICHOT 23, PP. 185–186

"בית המדרש" איז אן ארט וואו מ'לערנט תורה צוזאמען (ניט אן ארט וואו אידן פארזאמלען זיך צו הערן תורה, הלכה, דרשה וכיוצא בזה, פון א חכם), דאס הייסט, הגם אז אין בית המדרש איז פאראן א רב, ראש ישיבה וכיוצא בזה, און עס זיינען דא תלמידים . . . אף על פי כן, איז דער ענין פון בית המדרש, אז אלע "יושבי בית המדרש" זיינען זיך משתתף אין דעם לימוד: הערן די שאלה, שקלא וטריא אין איר וכו'.

דערפון איז אויך מובן אז שאלות וועלכע ווערן געפרעגט אין "בית המדרש" זיינען באופן שונה ווי די שאלות וואס מען פרעגט במקום ישיבת בית דין, דיין, ביי א רב: בשעת מ'פרעגט א שאלה ביי בית דין, דיין, א רב, אפילו ווען דערביי שטייען תלמידים, איז מובן אז די שאלה ווערט געפרעגט דוקא ביי בית דין.

מה שאין כן א שאלה וואס ווערט געפרעגט בבית המדרש, איז זי געווענדעט (ניט צום ראש בית המדרש, ראש ישיבה, וכיוצא בזה, נאר) צו אלע "יושבי בית המדרש" – זיי זיינען אלע מעיין בהשאלה און יעדערער פון זיי קען זאגן דעתו בזה.

The study hall is where we study Torah together. It is not a place where Jews gather to hear a Torah lecture, a legal rendering, a sermon, etc. from a sage. This means that though there is a rabbi or a dean in the study hall as well as students, everyone is encouraged to participate. Everyone is a partner in the dialogue; they hear the question, they debate, etc.

This tells us that questions posed in a study hall are different from questions posed in a court, or in the private study of a rabbi or judge. When you pose a question in court or in a private study, the question is intended for the rabbi or judge even if the courtroom or study is filled with students.

When a question is posed in the study hall, it is not directed exclusively to the dean or teacher, rather it is addressed to everyone present. Everyone considers the question, and everyone is entitled to share an opinion.

The Common Thread

TEXT 12

THE REBBE, RABBI MENACHEM MENDEL SCHNEERSON, IBID., P. 188

דער חידוש אין די צוויי פרשיות איז, אז זיי זיינען נמשך און געזאגט געווארן מלמעלה דורך א טענה ובקשת המטה . . .

און דאס איז אויך די שייכות צו . . . "בבית המדרש היו יושבים" . . . מדגיש די חשיבות פון לימוד התורה על ידי המטה . . .

לימוד התורה בבית המדרש איז מדגיש די מעלת הלימוד דהאדם, המטה, מה שאין כן הקהלה (פתח אהל מועד – הערן דבר השם על ידי משה, הקהל את העם בשנת הקהל – הערן דבר השם על ידי המלך וכיוצא בזה) וואו ס'איז מודגש מעלת המעלה, די נקהלים זיינען בלויז שומעים ומקבלים הדברים.

ביז אז אי אפשר לבית המדרש בלא חידוש, דורך פלפול חברים וכו' ווערן נתחדש ענינים בתורה.

The novelty of these two stories is that the response only came from Above after a petition or a request was made here below. . . .

[Both stories] are associated with . . . the study hall . . . because both emphasize the importance of *our* Torah study. . . .

The atmosphere in the study hall emphasizes the importance of the student's study. This is unlike the large gathering place where the nation heard Moses lecture or the national gathering in the year of *Hakhel* to hear G-d's words spoken by the king. There, the emphasis was on the speaker. The role of the people was to listen and receive.

[The study hall is so different that] "Every session at a study hall stimulates a new insight" [Talmud, Chagigah 3a]. When colleagues argue and debate, etc., new Torah ideas rise to the surface.

KEY POINTS

» Repentance must be at the behest of the penitent. It is only when we turn back to G-d that G-d can tell us that we are welcome. Should G-d tell us before we are ready to hear it, we might not hear it.

» Some things in life can be learned from a book or from others. Some things in life can only be learned from personal experience. Marriage, parenting, and grief are but a few examples.

» The realization of how much we treasure G-d can only be arrived at from personal experience. When we have experienced distance, we learn to cherish closeness.

» Our relationship with G-d is the gist of Judaism. We can learn the laws and traditions of Judaism from others. But the heart of Judaism must be learned from personal experience.

» We learn the hows and whys in a lecture hall. The teacher lectures and we listen. We *experience* Judaism in the study hall. It is where we are encouraged to ask, propose, debate, and analyze until we internalize the teaching.

THE ROHR
Jewish Learning Institute

832 Eastern Parkway, Brooklyn, New York 11213

An affiliate of
Merkos L'Inyonei Chinuch
The Educational Arm of the Worldwide Chabad-Lubavitch Movement

The Jewish Learning Multiplex

Brought to you by the Rohr Jewish Learning Institute

In fulfillment of the mandate of the Lubavitcher Rebbe, of blessed memory, whose leadership guides every step of our work, the mission of the Rohr Jewish Learning Institute is to transform Jewish life and the greater community through the study of Torah, connecting each Jew to our shared heritage of Jewish learning.

While our flagship program remains the cornerstone of our organization, JLI is proud to feature additional divisions catering to specific populations, in order to meet a wide array of educational needs.

THE ROHR JEWISH LEARNING INSTITUTE

A subsidiary of Merkos L'Inyonei Chinuch,
the adult educational arm of the Chabad-Lubavitch movement

Torah Studies provides a rich and nuanced encounter with the weekly Torah reading.

Jewish teens forge their identity as they engage in Torah study, social interaction, and serious fun.

The Rosh Chodesh Society gathers Jewish women together once a month for intensive textual study.

TorahCafe.com provides an exclusive selection of top-rated Jewish educational videos.

Participants delve into our nation's past while exploring the Holy Land's relevance and meaning today.

This yearly event rejuvenates mind, body, and spirit with a powerful synthesis of Jewish learning and community.

Equips youths facing adulthood with education and resources to address youth mental health.

Select affiliates are invited to partner with peers and noted professionals, as leaders of innovation and excellence.

MyShiur courses are designed to assist students in developing the skills needed to study Talmud independently.

This rigorous fellowship program invites select college students to explore the fundamentals of Judaism.

A crash course that teaches adults to read Hebrew in just five sessions.

Machon Shmuel is an institute providing Torah research in the service of educators worldwide.

Made in United States
North Haven, CT
29 April 2023